AUTHOR	CLASS
CAPPELLI, T.	C051

TITLE

The Furness trail

Published by Sigma Leisure – an imprint of
Sigma Press, 1 South Oak Lane, Wilmslow, Cheshire SK9 6AR, England.

British Library Cataloguing in Publication Data
A CIP record for this book is available from the British Library.

ISBN: 1-85058-328-5

05905527

Typesetting and Design by: Sigma Press, Wilmslow, Cheshire.

Maps and photographs: by the author

Cover photograph: Coniston Water, Beverly Bates

Printed by: Manchester Free Press

General Disclaimer

Whilst every effort has been made to ensure that the information given in this book is correct, neither the publisher nor the author accept any responsibility for any inaccuracy.

PREFACE

Let me ask you a question. Why do people walk? The simple answer is to get from A to B and before cars and trains this was the main reason one walked. Today, however, most people walk for the pleasure of the walk itself rather than to get anywhere. A bit like Chris Bonington's reason for climbing Everest, "because it's there", people walk not because there is anything for them at the end of the walk, but to be able to say "I did it". This is particularly true of long distance walks. Thousands of people walk the Coast to Coast from St. Bees to Robin Hood's Bay each year. But is there anything to do at Robin Hood's Bay once you get there, other than turn around and go home? Wainwright says "one should always have a definite objective in a walk as in life". How true, but how much better if the objective is more than just finishing.

It was with this in mind that I devised this book. Many times I have completed a walk where I have enjoyed the scenery, the countryside and sometimes even the company but on finishing have thought, is that it? Instead I wanted a walk where I knew that on reaching my destination there was something to see or do, or which gave me the time to study places I had passed.

The result is The Furness Trail. Essentially a long distance circular walk, it will, I hope, provide you with something more. Walking with a purpose - a means to an end. I like to think of it as a new departure in long distance walking. How does it work? Let me explain. The walk is divided into seven days, each day ending at a small town or village in South Lakeland. Each day's walk is described in the Walk Day Chapters and each is relatively short. This gives you time to take in the changing views and explore anything of interest along the way. At the end of each day's walk you can find accommodation and are encouraged to take the next day off to explore the various attractions of the town and its surrounding area. This is the purpose of the Tour Day Chapters which describe not only the town or village you are staying in, but also nearby places of interest and activities and events which you could take part in. Each attraction is described in some detail, together with instructions on how to get there and opening times. Using this information you can decide where, if anywhere, you would like to visit. For instance, you could walk the Trail from Levens to Cartmel and spend the next day visiting Holker Hall. The day after, you would carry on to Newby Bridge where you would go abseiling. In this way you can combine walking and sightseeing in a myriad of combinations providing you with plenty of options.

"What?", I hear the purists cry, "take a day off on a long distance walk? Go sightseeing? Be a tourist? Heaven forbid.". If that's how you feel, then fine. The Trail is a beautiful and interesting walk of 73 miles in its own right and can be done easily in seven days. On the other hand you could extend the walk to fourteen days or longer by really exploring the area using this book as your guide. The Furness Trail then becomes not just a long distance walk but more of - dare I say it - a holiday.

In Furness you have the perfect setting for such a walk as this. Firstly, you have the beautiful landscape through which to walk. Lying between the Lakeland mountains to the north and the shores of Morecambe Bay to the south, this area of South Cumbria is often neglected and passed over by people heading for the more dramatic and wilder fells of Lakeland. However, it is equally beautiful and often just as dramatic and though much of the Trail lies within the National Park, many of the paths and tracks used are overlooked by most walkers. In fact it is unlikely that you will see many people at all on the actual walks, apart from the odd local, who are friendly enough and only too willing to share their knowledge of the area with you. The area also reeks of history which is told as a story by its many buildings and monuments, echoing its changing fortunes through time. There are prehistoric settlements, priories from the time when most of the land belonged to the monks of Furness Abbey, pele towers from the period when the Scots were continually raiding, large halls of statesmen farmers and here and there the evidence of industry both past and present. Furness also holds attractions for the more energetic of you such as horse riding, water sports and mountain biking. Something for everyone is an over-used phrase, but one which really could apply to Furness and the South Lakes.

The seven towns and villages were chosen to provide accommodation and a convenient place to explore the surrounding area from. They range in size and activity from the almost sleepy little village of Levens to the hustle and bustle of Bowness. Each has its own character and each will appeal more to some than to others. I have my favourite town on the walk, my wife has hers and I am sure you will have yours. The main thing is that with this guide you should be able to enjoy each town in your own way. You could start the walk at any of these towns, since the walk is circular and where you start on the circle is unimportant. I have started from Kendal, with the first day's walk from Kendal to Levens. This is because Kendal is easy to get to by both car and public transport and for most people, it will be the first of the seven towns you come to. In choosing the local places to visit in each Tour Day, I have tried to keep them within walking distance so that this really can be a walking holiday. Directions and maps are included for each entry as are opening times. I also wanted to include an idea of price, though realised actual figures would soon be out of date. Instead I have indicated the cost by grouping them into bands. These are as follows:-

A - below £2.50   D - £10.00 to £15.00
B - £2.50 to £5.00   E - £15.00 to £20.00
C - £5.00 to £10.00   F - over £20.00

(These are at prices in 1992 and are per person)

Enjoy the walk but most of all enjoy what you get out of the walk. As W.H.Davies, the Lakeland poet, once said, "A poor life this if, full of care, We have no time to stand and stare." So stand and stare for a while. You might enjoy it!

Lastly, my thanks go to the many people who helped me with the Trail. Firstly, Nigel Kelly from the National Park who helped me check the rights of way; to Bev and Jon Bates who provided a bed, food (such as it was!) and help with the title; to Martyn Walker for advice on the birds and finally to Andrea who walked every step with me, supported and chastised me, but never complained. Even when chased by a cow.

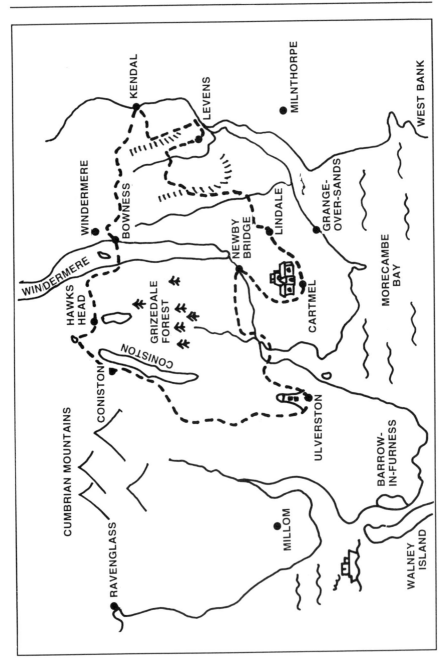

CONTENTS

INTRODUCTION

I have to be honest, this book has the wrong title. It shouldn't really be called *The Furness Trail*, but to be properly accurate it should be named The Furness, Cartmel and Old Westmorland Trail. However, since this is a little unwieldy and probably would not fit on the front cover, The Furness Trail is adequate. After all, the Furness Way has only 22 miles of its 75 mile length actually in Furness, so why can't the Furness Trail wander out of Furness?

Many people are confused by Furness and are not exactly sure where it is. They have heard of Barrow-in-Furness and even Broughton-in-Furness, but that's about all. Well let me set the record straight. The boundary of Furness, as officially set by the Abbot of Furness Abbey in 1157, is all the land between the River Duddon as far as Wrynose Pass and the River Leven and Windermere as far as the River Brathy. So Furness is not just the peninsula between the two estuaries of the Duddon and the Leven, but all the fells, tarns and woods in a great rectangle bounded in the north by the Little Langdale Valley. This means that many of the Lake District's most famous spots are within Furness. Coniston, Hawkshead and Claife Heights are all part of Furness's rich and varied country and all these places are visited on the Trail. However, to have a walk in just Furness would be a little limiting, especially since there are so many other wonderful places on its doorstep. For this reason the Trail also threads its way through the old parish of Cartmel, which together with Furness made up an outpost of Lancashire before it all became Cumbria, and also through parts of old Westmorland.

But this is supposed to be an introduction to the area through which you will be walking, so whether Furness, Cartmel, Lancashire, Westmorland or Cumbria, the fact remains that this area is a historical and geological goldmine with a past which has shaped the present landscape to a mixture of rolling, wooded fells, dramatic limestone cliffs and small, traditional towns.

Let's start at the beginning with the geology of the area. Around 400 million years ago the whole of the Lake District was a seething inferno of active volcanoes spewing out liquid rock. This cooled to form the large, craggy mountains which are the heart of the District. Following this period of volcanic activity, earthquakes caused water to flood much of the area forming warm, shallow seas. It was within these seas that the two main rocks of the area were formed. First, as the new mountains eroded, the material was washed down into the seas and gradually compressed to form the hard, grey Silurian Slates which now form the main part of the southern Lakes. Then, as the seas warmed, they became populated with millions of small creatures. As these creatures died their skeletons began to pile up on the seabed forming a thin layer of limestone rock. Over several million years the seas retreated and the area underwent more upheaval, pushing it upwards into a rough dome shape, capped with the layer of limestone under which lay the slate.

Then came the Ice Age. Massive glaciers covered the land and literally scrubbed off the top of the dome, exposing the Silurian Slate and leaving only fragments of the limestone in the east and south of the region. When the ice retreated it left large, flooded valleys which became the lakes of the Lake District. In the south of the District the slate was formed into gentle, rounded hills surrounded by a thin fringe of limestone. This is how the area stands today. The acid soil of the slate supports great tracts of woodland and in between are giant outcrops of limestone, forming the dramatic escarpments and pavements of Whitbarrow and Hampsfell. This mixture of wood and limestone was to have a great effect on south Lakeland's later history.

Man arrived in the area not long after the ice had retreated and the remains of many prehistoric settlements are to be found in the region. When the Romans arrived at the end of the 1st century, they found a very primitive people in small, scattered settlements. The Romans left their own mark on the area in the form of forts at Kendal and Hardknott as well as the straight Roman roads. It was the Romans who probably first used Morecambe Sands as a main route between this area and

Lancaster. The departure of the Romans left a certain void which was not really filled until the coming of the Vikings in the 8th century. These Norse settlers came via the Isle of Man and Ireland and brought stability and extensive farming to the area. Their legacy can be seen in most of the place-names which exist in this region. Thwaite for instance is a common ending in the Lake District and is the Norse word for a clearing in the forest. For this is what many of the settlers did, clear patches of forest and establish farms and settlements. Other Norse words include fell, booth, gill and beck.

In 1066 came the Normans, though they did not reach this part of their new kingdom until the end of the century. The first half of the next century saw many Norman buildings springing up and many of the area's churches, villages and market towns originate from this time. The Normans' biggest impression on the area, however, was made by the setting up of Furness Abbey in 1127 by King Stephen. A decade or so earlier Henry I had established the le Fleming family as military overlords in Furness in order to quash any rebellions and the area was, as modern planners would say, ripe for development. The Furness monks achieved this by replacing the small sheep farms with the largest sheep runs in Europe and by developing the small iron industry which existed into a major iron exporter. The iron industry was particularly important in shaping the countryside. At this time iron was smelted using large amounts of charcoal, together with iron ore in primitive bloomeries. Furness had an abundance of wood to produce charcoal together with nearby limestone which was later used to extract impurities in smelting and it is not surprising that the iron industry survived for many years in this part of the world. This helped preserve the great expanses of woodland which still exist in this area by preventing them being used for agriculture. Instead the demand for charcoal maintained a standard and coppice system of woodland management which preserved the woods in a near natural state. Evidence of such woods and of the iron industry as a whole will be seen many times on the Trail.

In addition to Furness Abbey, the smaller priory of Cartmel was also established in the 12th century and together these two religious houses ruled the area for several centuries. During the 13th and 14th centuries the Lake District as a whole was continually subjected to border raids from the Scots and this led to the building of pele towers. These were massive towers of three or four stories linked to the houses of wealthy families who would take refuge in the tower during a raid. Many of these towers can still be seen, though many have now been incorporated into large mansions such as Sizergh Castle.

The next big change came in 1536 with the Dissolution of the monasteries by Henry VIII. On his orders the Abbeys were demolished and stripped of their lands by the Crown who then sold it back to the tenant farmers at inflated prices. These farmers became known as Yeoman or Statesmen Farmers and were the new lords of the land. Iron smelting and other industries, no longer under the control of the monks, continued to flourish with large, new blast furnaces springing up at places like Backbarrow.

The Union of Scotland and England in 1603 brought relief from the Scottish raiders and the Enclosures Act at the end of the 18th century saw the building of the great stone walls which stretch across much of this land. It was also about this time that the Industrial Revolution saw a shift in iron production to the coalfields of the Midlands and although

On the Trail to Cartmel

many woodsmen diversified into gunpowder and bobbin making, the heyday of South Lakeland's woodlands were over.

The land has changed little since then with only the introduction of the odd new factory such as Glaxo, making an impression. Farming remains the main way of life in these parts and the landscape reflects this. Tourism, a relatively new prospect in this area, has seen many people come into the area but they come because of the way it is and hopefully will remain and have little wish to see any change. So this beautiful part of the country will, I hope, always remain so and if this Trail allows you to see the marvellous scenery and delve into its past then both of us will have been rewarded.

WALK DAY 1:
KENDAL TO LEVENS

Route: Kendal – Scout Scar – Helsington Church – Sizergh Castle – Levens Park – Levens.

Distance: 8 miles.

Maps: 1:50,000 O.S. Landranger No. 97 Kendal to Morecambe or 1:25,000 O.S. Outdoor Leisure English Lakes S.E. and 1:25,000 O.S. Pathfinder No. 627 Milnthorpe

Getting There: Kendal lies at the junction of many main roads, including the A6 and A65. Most people arriving by car get there via Junction 36 of the M6, then by following the A591 to the town. There are several places to park, though if you wish to leave your car for more than a day, the only safe overnight parking is down by the river. It is also free and for this reason gets full very quickly.

There are many buses to and from Kendal and it has its own train station on the branch line from Oxenholme. One of the main buses is the 555 which runs between Lancaster and Keswick via all the towns along the A591. This service also calls at Levens Bridge, so you could complete today's walk then return to Kendal on this bus if you wish.

The Walk

The distance from Kendal to Levens as the proverbial crow flies is around $3^{1}/_{2}$ miles. However, taking a more circuitous route promotes today's walk up to 8 miles and gives us the chance to see the beautiful and often dramatic landscape of this area. You will certainly find Scout Scar dramatic and it comes as an unexpected pleasure to those who think of this area as soft, rolling hills. The views from the Scar are second to few. We then meander along the edge of the Scar to

Helsington church and Sizergh Castle. Today's relatively short walk means we have plenty of time to explore these fascinating buildings if we wish, before making our way through the wooded Levens Park to Levens Bridge. From there it is a cock-stride across the fields to the village of Levens itself. I cannot think of a nicer or more gentle way to start a long distance walk.

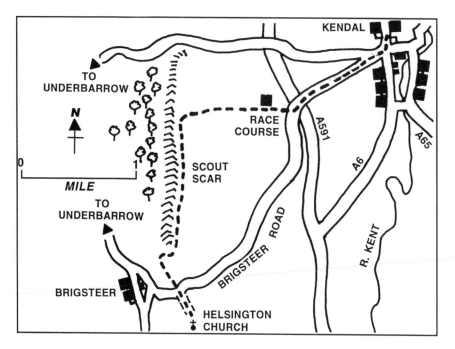

Section 1: Kendal to Helsington Church

Start the walk from Kendal Tourist Information Centre, which is on the main street, Stricklandgate. From here follow the road opposite (All Hallows Lane), uphill as it becomes Beast Banks. Continue uphill until you reach the sign for Underbarrow and Scout Scar by the 'phone box.

On your way up Beast Banks you will pass the site of Kendal's first castle. Not as big or as famous as the stone castle across the river, this was a motte and bailey affair built by Ketel de Tailbois in 1092. It stood for 100 years before being abandoned in favour of a much bigger stone castle, the ruin of which can still be seen towering over the town. The original site of the castle is now marked only by a flat green and a small knoll, on top of which stands an equally small obelisk dedicated to liberty.

Continue straight ahead at the sign, past the small green and up Brigsteer Road. Follow this road for half a mile until it crosses the dual carriageway. 100 yards after crossing the carriageway, turn right between two stone pillars by Kendal Racecourse. Follow the lane up to the farmyard and to the left of the buildings. Walk by the wall on your right to a metal kissing gate. Go through and follow the path by the wall, across the fell until it reaches another kissing gate.

This is the back of Scout Scar, a massive limestone escarpment lying along the edge of the Lyth Valley. The fields here are covered in typically bright coloured calcareous flowers which provide food for a whole host of equally bright butterflies. Walk across this fell in high summer, as I did, and the colour and spectacle of the butterflies is pure serendipity.

Two of the most numerous included the Common Blue and the six-spot Burnet, the latter being a day-flying moth. The food plant of both these is the birds-foot trefoil, a small, yellow pea-like flower and it is no surprise to see this creeping plant scattered across the fell in some numbers. The small windswept bushes which are also dotted across the grassland are juniper. Used in the making of gin, its berries have that distinctive smell which makes you think of ice and tonic water. They do have other uses though and are said to sweeten the breath if chewed. Another aromatic plant which is common on this limestone ridge is wild thyme. This is not something your teenage son has at parties, but a small creeping plant once highly valued for its medical properties. It can be used for sore throats, colds and even flatulence.

Go through the gate and take the path straight ahead to the edge of the escarpment – Scout Scar. Turn left and follow the path along the edge of the ridge for half a mile until you reach a large cairn and a junction of paths.

This massive limestone ridge towers above the Lyth Valley like some stranded sea-cliff with the flat fields of the Lyth lapping its feet. The view from here is mighty indeed and it is said that John Martin the artist painted The Plains of Heaven from this spot. Here is your first view of Morecambe Bay, with its wide, level sands and mud flats reaching out towards Arnside and the Lancashire coast. The Bay will became a familiar sight before the end of the Trail.

The View from Scout Scar

At the cairn continue straight ahead on the path following the escarpment edge as it slowly descends to meet a wall at the bottom of the scar. Continue on the path, with the wall on your right, to a wooden gate. Pass through the gate and follow the track on the other side to the road. Turn right and along the road for 70 yards to a sharp bend. Here turn left over the cattle grid and take the track to Helsington church. Note the poem dedicated to the church by Wordsworth, here by the cattle grid, before following the track down to the church.

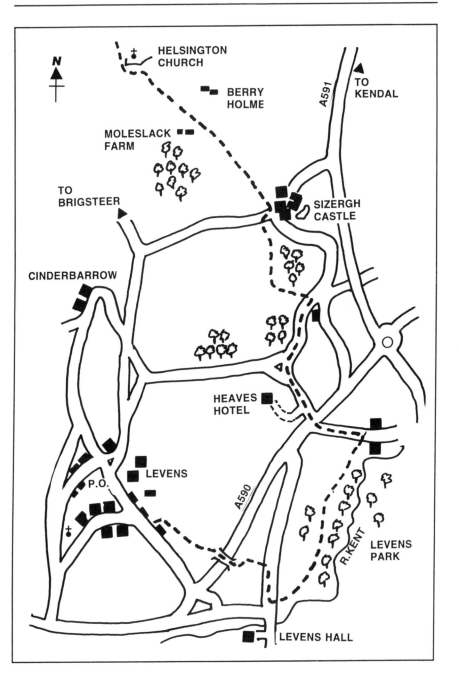

Section 2: Helsington Church to Levens

The church of St. John serves only around 300 people in the ancient parish of Helsington and the regular congregation numbers just ten. However, the church is well loved and cared for and looks out on the nicest view of any church in the land. It is certainly worth a look inside for it has a beautiful simplicity which enhances the fine view outside. In fact the scene outside is also depicted inside in the form of an angelic mural by Mason D'Aumaret. The church itself was built in 1726, the site chosen for its association with outdoor worship during the Middle Ages. Even if you do not venture inside, take time out to sit on one of the benches under the trees and take in the landscape.

After passing the church turn immediately left up the track signed for Berry Holme. Follow the tarmac lane until it runs between two walls. Here turn off to the right, heading for the right -hand side of the trees ahead. Walk past the trees to the ladder stile. After the stile, walk downhill to a gate onto a lane. Turn left on the lane to follow it through the gate and along the track to the barn. Continue past the barn for another 300 yards to a wooden gate at a bend. Go straight ahead, through the gate, and follow the track towards Sizergh Castle. Pass under the power lines to the gate onto the lane.

From this point, Sizergh Castle is up the lane to the left. You could visit the Castle now if you wish and have the time, or you could visit on your sightseeing day tomorrow. If you are not planning on spending tomorrow sightseeing, then it is definitely worth taking a look at now. Off you go then!

I will not say anything about the Castle here, since it is all explained in the next chapter. I will, however, take this opportunity to mention Thomas West who lived at Sizergh and died in the Castle in 1779. Thomas West wrote one of the first and most famous guides to the Lake District called, predictably, *Guide to the Lakes*. This became the bible of early tourists and West certainly waxed lyrically on the area. He recommended several view points from where to see the District at its best and to really 'do the Lakes', one had to visit each of these spots in turn. We shall pass a few of these spots on the rest of the Trail. However, to truly do the views justice, one had to be equipped with a telescope to view 'inaccessible rocks' and a landscape mirror, "Plano-convex glasses to remove objects great and near to a due distance and obtainable from any optician". Try getting one of those at Boots.

The Swans at Sizergh Castle

If you are not visiting the castle, turn right on the lane and then turn left into the car-park. Walk across the car-park, keeping to the right, and along the track on the far side. In front of the gateway with a no entry sign turn right to a wooden gate and stone steps. Go over the steps and follow the path by the wall to two gates on the opposite side of the field. Go through the gate on the left and then turn left to follow the wall on your left hand side. This leads downhill to the corner of the field and a stile onto a track. Turn left on the track and follow it down to the road. In front of you here, is the back of the Strickland Arms, providing good Yorkshire beer and a pleasant garden to sit out in. This provides good opportunity for a rest and is worth the stop. After-all, not many good things come from Yorkshire!

On the road behind the pub turn right and follow it for a quarter of a mile to a road junction.

Walking along this lane you will notice the many plants growing along the roadside. Amongst them is our only native fern with non-divided fronds – the Hart's Tongue fern. It's not difficult to see how it got its name, with its long, strap-shaped fronds, coming to a point at the tip. In Victorian times cultivating ferns was a popular pastime, since they were about the only thing that would grow in the cold, damp houses of the time. The Victorians could not nip down to Sainsbury's for their plants, but would take them from the wild instead. Hart's Tongue fern was one of the more popular and specimens with fronds which forked at the tip were particularly prized. So, watch out for one!

Turn left at the junction, then left again following the sign for Kendal. Continue to the main road (A590). The Heaves Hotel, here on your right, is one of the places to stay at near Levens. (See next chapter.) Taking care, cross the main road and go down the lane opposite (Force Lane). Follow this for a quarter of a mile to the farm and a metal signpost for Levens Bridge.

At the sign turn right through the gate to follow the path towards the trees and steps. Go over the steps and continue by the trees on the left to some stone steps by a black gate. Go over the steps and into Levens Park. Follow the yellow arrows straight ahead and then right on the clear path. Follow the path through the park for half a mile to the road at Levens Bridge (A6).

Levens Park was created as the noble deer Park of Levens Hall and is still grazed by black fallow deer and Bagot goats, named after the present occupants of Levens Hall. Thomas West thought highly of Levens Park and called it "one of the sweetest spots that fancy can imagine". It does, however, have an earlier history and in the early 1970s archeologists discovered two stone circles in the Park together with flint knives and fragments of beakers. It is believed a large farm settlement was built here on the site of a prehistoric stone works. The Park even has its own legend and it is said that a traveller of 200 years ago put a curse on the place after being refused refreshment at the Hall. No male heirs would be born to Levens Hall until the river ran dry and a white stag was to be seen in the Park. The curse continued until 1895 when the river froze and a white, male fawn was spotted in the Park. The following year Alan Bagot was born. Today, a white stag seen in the Park is thought to predict any important event.

If you wish to visit Levens Hall now, the entrance is 100 yards down the road, to the left. For more information see the next chapter. If continuing to Levens Village, turn right, up the road (signed dead end) for 200 yards to a metal signpost for Levens. Turn left to follow the sign along the track. This leads you over a footbridge across the dual carriageway and into a field. Go over the ladder stile and straight ahead to another ladder stile. Go over this before bearing left on the path towards the houses. Pass through a metal gate and along a short track to the road. Turn right on the road and into the village.

TOUR DAY 1: LEVENS

Levens Hall

Accommodation

Unlike the rest of the villages along the Trail, Levens doesn't really cater for tourists and so few places of accommodation exist in or around the village. The nearest to the centre is to the north-east of the village at Cinderbarrow. This is Birslack Grange, a comfortable guest house with reasonable rates.

Other than this there is the Heaves Hotel to the east of the village, which is larger and more expensive and the Wheatsheaf Hotel, a country pub in Brigsteer, a mile and a half to the north. Alternatively, you could stay

at Low Plain Farm
which is not only a
farm park but also
provides pleasant
accommodation for
the weary. The farm
and how to get to it
is described further
on.

Birslack Grange,
Cinderbarrow,
Levens. Tel. (05395)
60989
Heaves Hotel,
Levens, Nr. Kendal.
Tel. (05395) 60396
Wheatsheaf Hotel,
Brigsteer, Nr. Ken-
dal Tel.(04488) 254
Low Plain Farm,
Brigsteer, Nr. Ken-
dal Tel. (04488) 323

LEVENS

The first thing you
notice of Levens vil-

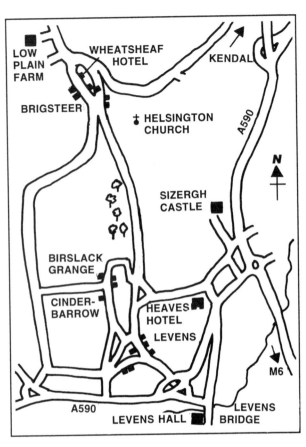

lage, whether walking to it or approaching in the car, is the impressive
church spire of St. John the Evangelist which according to one writer
"gleams like a pillar of salt in the evening light". This may or may not
be true. What is true is the fact that the spire, like most of the houses in
this small and peaceful village, is constructed of limestone taken from
the surrounding fells.

Levens village remains a quiet residential village lying between the A590
and the A6 and therefore by-passed by most traffic. It was once,
however, very different, with the village an important stage in the local
road network situated, as it was, at the end of the original causeway
across the marshes of the Lyth Valley. The building of the causeway

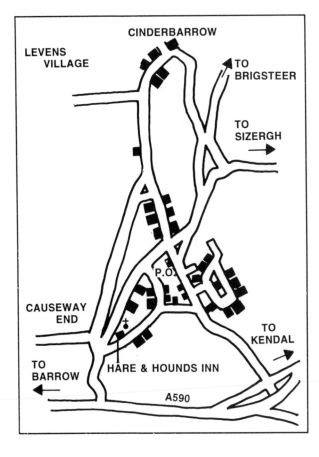

allowed travellers from Lancashire to west Cumbria to cross this otherwise unpassable area in relative safety. Alternatively they took their chances across the sands of Morecambe Bay. In fact, the southern end of Levens village, around the church, still retains the name of Causeway End, if only on the map.

Being a residential village there is little to see in the village itself, although the church is worthy of a short visit if only to see its unusual bells. The church was commissioned in 1829 by the then occupant of Levens Hall, Mary Howard. In 1913 the parishioners of Levens decided that their church should have bells and bought three large cast iron bells from Milnthorpe. However, the church was not built to take bells and they would not fit into the building. Instead, the bells were hung outside in the churchyard under a small, slate-roofed shelter. As if this wasn't enough, the bells will never ring anyway, for they have no clappers!

LEVENS HALL

In 1170 William de Lancaster granted a charter giving land to Norman de Hieland. The De Hielands became the De Redmans and around 1300

Mathew de Redman built the first Levens Hall on this granted land. This first hall had a large pele tower to defend it from Scottish raiders and it is the remains of this hall, including the pele tower, which forms the oldest part of Levens Hall today. The present impressive mansion was built in 1580 by the Bellingham family who had bought the original Hall from the de Redmans around 20 years earlier. James Bellingham made many later additions to the house including fine oak panelling and plasterwork, which can still be seen to this day. In fact the house still stands much as it did when it was built, a fine example of an Elizabethan mansion with lots to see both inside and out.

In 1688 the last Bellingham (the Hall suffered throughout its history from a lack of male heirs due to the traveller's curse) sold the house to Col. James Graham. In 1692 Col. Graham employed the services of Monsieur de Beamount, the King's gardener and designer of Hampton Court gardens, to lay out and design the gardens for Levens Hall. The result is one of the best gardens to be seen anywhere including some of the most famous topiary outside Hampton Court. Some of these sculptured hedges are truly monumental whilst many are just puzzling, but all are worth seeing. As well as the topiary the gardens have many herbs and unusual plants on show and some are even for sale at the garden entrance, so those which impress you can be bought and planted in your own garden back home.

Inside the house the attractions are no less worthy. In addition to the wood panelling and Italian plasterwork of James Bellingham, there is a fine collection of Jacobean furniture, Spanish leather coverings and the earliest example of English patchwork in existence. There are many beautiful paintings, a small collection of Cromwellian armour together with personal items of Napoleon, Wellington and Nelson. These many items reflect Levens Hall long and turbulent history, passing from family to family by marriage or sale to the ownership of the Bagot family who still occupy part of the house today.

If the gardens or historic house do not tempt you to Levens Hall, then maybe the steam engines will. Next to the Hall, are laid out a collection of working steam engines of all sizes and on Sundays they fire-up the full size traction engines including a magnificent steam organ which plays away tirelessly in the car park.

There is plenty to see and take in at Levens Hall and you could spend virtually a full day there if you explore both house and garden. There is a tearoom where you can buy light lunches and drinks as well as a gift shop and a picnic site if you want to take your own lunch. The Hall even boasts three ghosts; a pink lady, a black dog and a grey lady who haunts the gardens. So whether inside the house or out in the gardens, beware!

Getting There: The easiest way to get to Levens Hall is on foot and this is simply done by retracing your steps of yesterday and the main walk, back to the A6 and Levens Bridge. The entrance to the Hall is a matter of yards from the bridge and only 1 mile from the centre of Levens.

Opening Times: The Hall opens to the public from Easter until the end of September, every day except Fridays and Saturdays. Opening times are 11.00 a.m. to 5.00 p.m. with the steam collection on view from 2.00 p.m. to 5.00 p.m.. Telephone Sedgewick (05395) 60321.

Admission: There are two admission rates. One for the house and garden (band B) and one for the gardens only (band A). Both are reasonable and value for money.

SIZERGH CASTLE

Sizergh Castle and Levens Hall have one thing at least in common. Both are built around an ancient pele tower. However, unlike Levens Hall which has passed from family to family, Sizergh has always been home to the Strickland family, although the castle now actually belongs to the National Trust.

Sizergh comes from a Norse word meaning 'Sigarith's dairy farm' and the land here was sold to the Strickland family in 1239. The pele tower, the largest still standing in Cumbria, was built a hundred years later. In 1540 the Great Hall was added completing this magnificent Elizabethan mansion, finished about the time work on Levens began. They therefore make an interesting comparison. Like Levens, Sizergh also has some fine oak panelling. As you enter the Great Hall you will notice the carved screen of panelling made around 1555. The workmanship on this screen is so great that it is thought to have been carried out by French or Dutch workmen or possibly Englishmen who learnt their art abroad. The Hall, as in the house as a whole, is a treasure chest of early English furniture

Ivy Clad Sizergh Castle

such as an ancient oak chest and refectory table. The upper hall contains portraits of the Strickland family who have played an important part in English history. There was a Strickland at Hastings in 1066, at the Battle of Agincourt and at Edgehill.

Other rooms include the Queen's Room, so called because of a carved inscription above the fireplace which states '1569 Viv at Regina'. This also contains beautiful panelling and furniture as does the drawing room and the morning room. If all these room names are confusing you, then wait until you get to the Inlaid Chamber. This room is so called because of the intricate inlaid panelling dating from 1568. However, the panelling is no longer in the room but 250 miles away in the Victoria and Albert Museum to whom it was sold in 1890. The room does, however, contain the original stucco ceiling and frieze. There are many other rooms to wander around, all containing some beautiful furniture and various personal items collected by the Stricklands through the ages.

Once outside the house the gardens are equally beautiful and provide the perfect setting for the impressive, ivy-covered pele tower. Mainly laid out in the 18th century, the gardens include an attractive limestone rockery of ferns, a rose garden and a wild area. There is even a small pond with a pair of regal swans. Though not as big and as grand as Levens Hall the gardens are cool and pleasant and worth visiting, whilst the house itself gives you another glimpse into Elizabethan England.

Getting There: From Levens Village the easiest and most pleasant way to Sizergh Castle is by walking there. You could of course retrace your steps from yesterday, but this is rather a long way round and a much shorter route of just over 1 mile exists over Sizergh Fell.

With the post office in Levens behind you take the road straight ahead which leads north out of the village. Follow this for a quarter of a mile past 2 junctions on the left, to Heaves Farm and a metal signpost for Sizergh Castle. Turn left and follow the sign over the stone stile. Follow the clear track which bears right to a wooden gate in the wall.

When I did this walk one day in July this whole field was full of parked cars, people picnicking and couples strolling around. At the far end of the field stood a large group of people looking out over the wall. At first I was puzzled. What were these people doing? What were they looking at? What was going on? Then I noticed the Tote board and the flicking hands of the bookies. Not horse racing but a hound trail meeting. Meetings such as this are virtually a daily event in the Lake District and racing hounds is a popular pastime, especially for the bookies.

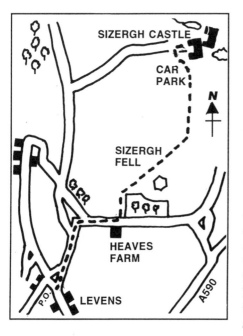

Trail hounds are much the same as fox hounds but are bred to be lighter and faster. They are tough dogs able to follow a trail over the roughest terrain and their owners are rightly proud of them. The sport is well organised and even has a ruling body dating back to 1906. Each race is usually held over 10 miles, having been laid out the day before by a couple of men with an aniseed soaked rag. The dogs are divided into three classes – puppies, under a year old; maidens, who have yet to win a prize; and seniors, which is open. Each race has a time limit of 45 minutes after which the race is void. This gives you an idea of how fast the dogs really are.

Go through the gate and bear half left to follow a faint track up hill to the opposite fence. At the gap in the fence pass into the next field and follow the track to the diagonally opposite corner of the field and stone steps by a gate. Go over the steps and follow the path ahead to more stone steps. Go over these and continue on the path into the car park and then into the Castle grounds and the ticket office.

Opening Times: Sizergh Castle is open from the beginning of April to the end of October from Sundays to Thursdays. However, it doesn't open until 1.30 p.m. so don't get there too early although the gardens and shop do open slightly earlier at 12.30 p.m. It all closes at 5.30 p.m. Telephone Sedgewick (05395) 60070.

Admission: There are two admission charges – one for the house and gardens (band B) and one for the gardens only (band A). Both are good value and slightly cheaper than Levens Hall, though the grounds are not so big. If you are a National Trust member remember to take your card.

LOW PLAIN FARM PARK

If you have ever wanted to get close to a pig, then this could be the place for you. If not a pig, then what about a goat, sheep or donkey? Low Plain Farm has all these and more.

Set around a traditional Cumbrian farm, this farm park allows members of the public to experience agriculture close up. Arranged around the farm are several paddocks and pens of various farm animals including many rare breeds – Jacob sheep, Bagot goats and a Gloucester Old Spot pig to name but a few. You can view all the animals and most are friendly enough to come up to you expecting to be fed. But be warned, the goats eat anything!

Most of the animals are in small paddocks scattered around the farm and there is a trail which takes you to each in turn. Many of the paddocks are open to visitors which gives you the chance to get 'hands on experience' of some of the animals. The site also includes a picnic site and a collection of old farm machinery such as some early Ferguson tractors. A display of smaller farm equipment is housed in the farm buildings. The hens and turkeys on the farm are entirely free-range. So much so that they are likely to follow you around the farm trail providing an ever close chatter of clucks and gobbles. For the younger children there is a pets' corner with guinea pigs and rabbits to be fussed and stroked.

The park is ideal for children but is interesting to all ages, particularly if you like animals or have an interest in agriculture.

It would not, however, occupy a full day on its own.

Getting There: Low Plain Farm Park is $2^1/_2$ miles north of Levens village and the only way there is on foot. So, a visit to the farm involves a 5 mile round trip, although if you are staying at Birslack Grange this is reduced by about a mile and if you are staying at Brigsteer, it is nearer than any of the other attractions. The walk from Levens to the farm is pleasant in itself, taking in the beginning of tomorrow's walk. The following directions should also be used to guide you to the accommodation in Brigsteer.

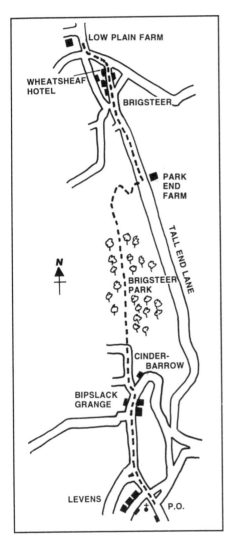

With the post office at Levens behind you, turn left to the crossroads by the Methodist church. Here go straight across and take the road opposite. Follow this road for a quarter of a mile to Cinderbarrow (Birslack Grange is here on the left). Continue past the houses of Cinderbarrow before turning left immediately after Inglewood Barn, a white house, down a track. Follow the public footpath sign for Park End along the track for 400 yards to a gate and stile into the woods. Go through the gate into the woods and follow the path straight ahead. The path leads through Brigsteer woods for half a mile until it meets another, wider track.

Brigsteer woods are owned and managed by the National Trust and, as the notice board at the entrance to the woods will tell you, they are being managed to increase the variety of plants and animals in the woods. They are achieving this by thinning the non-native trees and restoring the old coppice system, leaving the mature standards of oak, yew and lime. Many of the woods in this area are old coppice stands, once managed to supply the charcoal industry but now neglected. There will be a chance to see some good examples of such woods later on the Trail.

On the track turn left and follow it to a junction of paths after 500 yards. Again take the path on the left which leads to a ladder stile into a field. Cross the stile then straight ahead, roughly parallel with the wire fence to your left, until you reach an old track which zig-zags uphill to the diagonally opposite corner of the field. Go through the gate onto the lane and turn left along the lane for half a mile to the village of Brigsteer. Continue on the main road through the village, passing what used to be the post office, but like many rural post offices has been replaced by a post box. You should also look out for the natural spring on the right, set back slightly from the road. Above it is a sign declaring this as a public watering place of Helsington Parish. Here's your chance to make a fortune by bottling and selling it as 'Brigsteer Spa Water'!

At the end of the village is the Wheatsheaf Hotel and a road junction. Turn left at the junction and follow the road for one third of a mile to Low Plain Farm on the left.

Opening Times: The farm is open every day from Easter to mid October. It opens at 10.30 p.m. and closes at 5.00 p.m.

Telephone: Crosthwaite (05395) 68323

Admission: Admission prices to the farm are cheap (band A) and cover the whole park and its attractions.

If none of these attractions appeal then there are other places to visit further afield which involve catching a bus. All the following attractions are on, or near, the route of the 555 bus which runs from Keswick to Lancaster. To catch the bus you have to walk down to the A6 at Levens Bridge (see Levens Hall route) and catch the bus for Lancaster. There is a bus every hour during the week and every 2 hours on Sunday. It is best to check bus times first and you can ring Cumbrian buses on Kendal (0539) 733221.

HERON CORN MILL

This small museum combines a working corn mill and a paper making museum. Opened in 1975, the corn mill has been fully restored by the Beetham Trust. There has been a mill on this site for over 900 years and although the present mill dates from around 1730 it still grinds grain in the traditional way. The corn is ground between enormous mill stones which are driven by a 14 foot water wheel. This is powered by water shooting from a naturally occurring ledge of rock across the River Bela. The wheel also powers various other machines through a series of belts, cogs and line shafts all of which can be seen on the stone floor of the mill.

Next to the mill is the Mill Barn which in 1988 was converted into the Museum of Paper Making. This small museum traces the beginning of paper making and its development through history. Occasionally there are demonstrations of paper making by hand during which you can join in and make your own paper.

Though interesting on their own, the mill and museum are rather small and would not occupy a full day, but could be combined with a visit to nearby Milnthorpe, especially on a Friday which is market day.

Getting There: Heron Corn Mill is in Beetham, just south of Milnthorpe and as stated you need to catch the bus to Lancaster from Levens Bridge. Journey time from Levens is around 20 minutes. In Beetham follow the clear tourist signs to the mill.

Opening Times: The mill is open from April to September every day except Mondays. It opens at 11.00 a.m. and closes at 5.00 p.m.

Admission: Entrance to the paper making museum is free, but there is a small charge for the mill (band A).

LEIGHTON HALL

This is an 18th century 'Gothic' hall which is home to the Gillow family. Anybody who knows anything about furniture will recognise the name as fine makers of furniture and the house holds a fine collection of Gillow's work. It also contains the world's largest dolls house. The main attraction at Leighton Hall however, are the birds of prey which are flown free in the afternoon and put on a magnificent display.

Getting There: Leighton Hall lies a mile from the A6 at Yealand, half-way between Milnthorpe and Carnforth. Catch the bus to Lancaster from Levens Bridge – journey time is 30 mins. – then follow the brown tourist signs to Leighton Hall, heading west from the A6 at Yealand.

Opening Times: The Hall is open from May to September on Tuesdays to Fridays as well as Sundays and Bank Holiday Mondays. The Hall opens at 2.00 p.m. and closes at 5.00 p.m. with the bird displays at 3.30 p.m.

Tel. (0524) 734474

Admission: The entrance fee to the Hall is comparable with Levens Hall and Sizergh Castle (band A)

WALK DAY 2:
LEVENS TO CARTMEL

Route: Levens – Brigsteer – The Howe – Whitbarrow Scar – Witherslack Hall – Witherslack – Halecat – Lindale – Hampsfell – Cartmel.

Distance: 14 miles.

Maps: 1:50,000 O.S. Landranger No. 97 Kendal to Morecambe or 1:25,000 O.S. Pathfinder No. 627 Milnthorpe and 1:25,000 O.S. Pathfinder No. 636 Grange-over-Sands.

Getting There: Levens, a small residential village, is easy to get to by car lying as it does between the A591 and the A590. If coming from the M6, leave at junction 36 and follow the A591 towards Kendal. After 3 miles take the turning for the A590 to Barrow. Levens is signed to the right after about one mile. If following the A6 north, follow it as far as Levens Hall and the junction with the A590 then follow the signs for Levens Village.

The only way to Levens by public transport is by bus from Kendal. You could catch the 555 to Lancaster, get off at Levens Bridge and walk up to the village or you could catch one of the smaller buses which runs into the village itself. However, these are not as frequent although one of them (the 530/1/2) runs between Kendal and Ulverston via both Levens and Cartmel. To check bus times ring Kendal (0539) 733221.

The Walk

Today's walk is the longest and the most varied of the entire Trail. It starts by crossing the wide, flat marshes of the Lyth Valley before heading over the wooded tops of Whitbarrow to the edge of another limestone escarpment, Whitbarrow Scar. From here we join the Furness Way down the front of the Scar to Witherslack Hall before wandering through some ancient mixed woodland around the aptly named Yewbarrow. A small diversion from the Furness Way gives us a chance to linger a while in the gardens of Halecat House before rejoining it once more. This leads us to the small but thriving town of Lindale. After a small rest, perhaps in one of Lindale's two pubs, we start an easy climb onto the limestone pavement of Hampsfield Fell. This almost alien terrain comes to a head at the Hospice, a well-known and well-loved landmark which offers rest, shelter and a fine view across Morecambe Bay. Nestling below you is the tiny village of Cartmel with its square Priory towering above it like some mighty galleon. Who can resist such prospects?

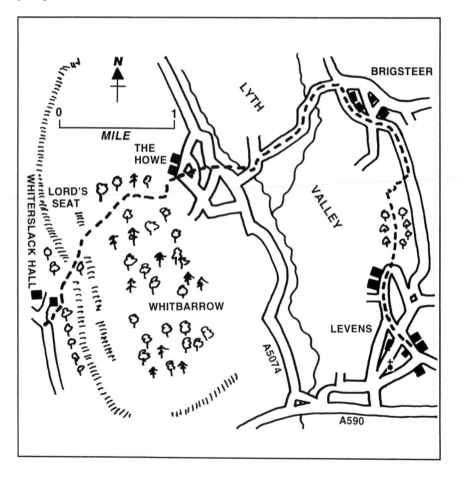

Section 1: Levens to Witherslack Hall

With the Post Office at Levens behind you, turn left to the crossroads by the Methodist Church. Here go straight across and take the road opposite. Follow this road for a quarter of a mile to Cinderbarrow (the starting point for those who stayed in Birslack Grange). Continue past the houses of Cinderbarrow before turning left immediately after Inglewood Barn, a white house, along a track. Follow the public footpath sign for Park End along the track for 400 yards to a gate and stile into the woods.

As you ramble up the track, Lyth Valley spreads out ahead of you offering fine views towards the hills beyond. Along the left of the track the edge of the wood is adorned with traveller's joy, draped carelessly across the various trees and shrubs. This plant is our only native clematis and was given the name of traveller's joy by Gerard, the great Elizabethan herbalist. Up until 1597 when Gerard wrote his famous herbal, the plant was known as viorna. Gerard obviously didn't take to this name and instead he noted the way the plant was to be found "decking and adorning ways and hedges where people travel" and he adds, "thereupon I have named it the traveller's joy".

Go through the gate into the woods and follow the path straight ahead. The path leads through Brigsteer woods for half a mile until it meets another, wider track.

The tall, purple headed flowers which you cannot fail to spot by the path are hemp agrimony. This is a common plant of marshes and wet woods and although the Latin name is *Eupatorium Cannabinum* don't bother trying to smoke it. You won't feel any better.

On the track turn left and follow it to a junction of paths after 500 yards. Again take the path on the left which leads to a ladder stile into a field. Cross the stile then straight ahead, roughly parallel with the wire fence to your left, until you reach an old track which zig-zags uphill to the diagonally opposite corner of the field. Go through the gate onto the lane and turn left. Follow the lane for half a mile to the road junction. At the junction turn left down the small lane which takes you behind the village of Brigsteer to a junction with a main road. (For those who stayed the night at the Wheatsheaf Hotel or Low Plain Farm this is your starting point.) Turn left, then left again after 20 yards down another small lane. Follow this lane for $1^1/_4$ miles as it makes its way across the flat valley floor, bending left then right, until you reach a third stone bridge over a ditch.

You are now crossing the wide stretches of the Lyth Valley. This flat, marshy valley is set on sedimentary rock trapped between the limestone escarpments of Scout Scar behind you and Whitbarrow Scar in front. To your left are the lower fields and marshes of the valley creeping out between the hills to meet the sands of Morecambe Bay. To the right, the valley reaches up between the small fells and hills around Underbarrow, forming a near perfect oblong. The strange thing about the Lyth Valley is its name. For a start, there is no River Lyth and the main river through the valley is the Gilpin, with Helsington and Underbarrow Pools at its upper levels. The second strange thing is that Lyth or Lythe is actually a Norse word meaning hillslope. Since this is one of the flattest areas around, with not so much as a hillslope in sight, this seems like a perculiar name to give such a valley.

The houses at The Howe

Just after the bridge is a public footpath sign on the right. Turn right by the sign over the ladder stile and along the top of the embankment. Cross four stiles to a gate onto the road. Turn right on the road and follow it uphill for 75 yards to a public footpath sign on the left. Go over the stile by the sign and following the wall on your right, walk uphill to a stile onto a lane. Take the lane straight ahead and uphill until it meets another lane. Here turn left then after 50 yards turn right along a track by Howe Fell cottage. Follow the track, taking the right fork at the public footpath sign, past the house until it leads between two stone pillars. Continue straight ahead along the path leading through oaks and yews until you come to a junction of tracks after 50 yards.

You are now entering the extensive woodland which covers the top of Whitbarrow like a crop of hair atop a newly cut Mohican. Like Scout Scar, Whitbarrow is another upthrust of limestone, left behind from the erosion of the 'dome' which once covered this area. However, it is much more impressive and dramatic than Scout Scar though in some ways less accessible being covered for most of its part by forest. Either way, it truly dominates the area and for anyone travelling along the A590 for the first time, the question is always, "What is that hill called?".

At the junction of paths turn left past an old millstone. There are several old quarries in this part of the fell and the millstone was probably one of the last products to come from the works, yet never delivered. Follow the path for 150 yards through yew and hazel coppice to a junction of paths and a yellow arrow. Follow the arrow left along a track to a gap in a wall. After the gap turn right following more yellow arrows to a gate into a field. In the field walk straight ahead to the far right hand corner and a stone stile with an iron grill. Cross this and then straight ahead on the path through the woods. The path leads through the trees for half a mile until it meets a much clearer path heading left to right.

Walking along this narrow path, the surrounding trees tower above you on both sides, closing you in and cutting out all views and landmarks. Within them you lose all sense of direction and time and it is easy to see how people can get lost within such woods, spending hours walking around in circles. However, there is no chance of that here provided that you follow these directions and so you can relax. Along this stretch of path there are many cypress trees. According to the old druids' calendar, I was born under the sign of the cypress tree which means I share similar characteristics with this tree. There are some very charismatic cypress trees about, don't you think?

On reaching the clearer path by a junction of arrows, turn left along the path. After just 10 yards you reach another junction of paths. Here turn right and continue through the woodland for 300 yards to a small cairn at a fork in the path. Take the left, clearer path climbing slowly uphill through birch and conifers for a quarter of a mile to another path leading left to right.

On the path turn right up to a stone stile in the wall. Cross the stile onto a grass-covered fell. Turn left along a path by the side of a small limestone 'cliff'. Follow the path which leads to a large cairn away to the right.

The Lord's Seat on Whitbarrow

This is Lord's Seat on the top of Whitbarrow. It is at this point that you join the route of the Furness Way which we shall follow, more or less, as far as Low Wood on the other side of Cartmel. This 75 mile, long distance walk takes the walker from Arnside in Lancashire to Ravenglass on the Cumbrian coast.

More importantly though are the impressive views down the Winster Valley and out towards Morecambe Bay. Not as dramatic, I feel, as Scout Scar where the ground drops suddenly and unnervingly away in front of you, the view is nonetheless impressive. The large cairn of Lord's Seat bears a plaque to Canon G.A.K Hervey, the founder of the Lake District Naturalist Trust. The cairn was raised especially in his memory and the surrounding fell makes up the Hervey Nature Reserve.

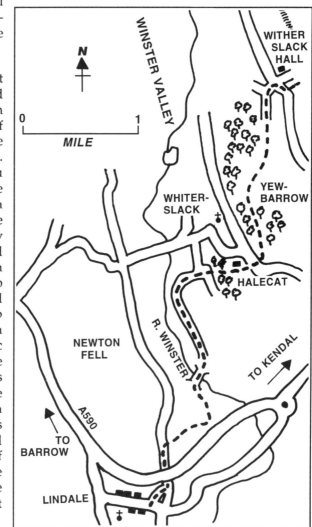

From Lord's Seat take the cairned path west, down the opposite side of the ridge from the one you came up. The path leads you downhill, before turning south along the ridge itself, until it finally reaches a stile and public footpath sign in the wall. Go over the stile and follow the steep path down through the trees to a public footpath sign at the bottom. Follow this to a gap in the wall. Go through the gap and across the football field (around the back of the goal) to a stile on the opposite side. Turn right after the stile to follow a track across the field to a gate by some farm buildings.

Whilst crossing the field it is worth stopping to look back at Whitbarrow Scar. It is from here that it looks its most impressive, the sheer limestone cliff towering above you and you can, perhaps, wonder how you managed to get from the top so easily.

Go through the gate and past the farm buildings to the lane by the entrance for Witherslack Hall School.

Section 2: Witherslack Hall to Lindale

Turn right on the lane, past the school entrance and on for 200 yards to a metal sign for Halecat. Turn left to follow the sign up a track which bends left after 50 yards between two high walls. After the gate by the farm houses, cross the field taking the right fork to the diagonally opposite corner of the field. Continue into the woods along the clear bridleway through towering ash and sycamore trees.

As I entered these woods one late October morning, I was greeted with a cacophony of chirps and whistles from hundreds of birds all around me. The sound continued to surround me as I wandered through the woods, though any sight of the birds remained an illusive glimpse. As I continued, the flocks would fly from my approach, always keeping about 20 feet ahead of me. When it comes to spotting birds I am no expert so I was at a loss to identify the dark shapes disappearing into the foliage. However, I am assured by my bird expert friend that they were a mixed flock of finches such as siskin, chaffinch and greenfinch all taking advantage of the abundant autumn fruits.

After a quarter of a mile the path leads out into bracken covered grassland and the path splits three ways. Take the path to the right, through the bracken to a wooden gate and stile on the opposite side of the field. Cross the stile and continue on the path through more woodland. Ignore paths off to the left and right and continue straight ahead through the trees for half a mile to the road at Witherslack.

This is Yewbarrow Fell and appropriately the woods contain many mature yew trees. The yew tree is one of only three native conifers which grow in Britain and they form some of the oldest woods in the country. The yew tree is another of those plants which gives rise to part of the English language. The species name for the yew is *Taxus* which comes from the Greek word *toxon* meaning bow, the wood of the yew having been used to make bows since classical times. Another well-known property of the yew tree is its powers of poison and the name *Taxus* gives us the English word toxic. So our word for poisonous actually comes from the Greek word for bow! Though deaths from eating yew are rare, it is still highly poisonous and death results from heart and breathing failure. It is said to be an antidote for adder bites, though I would imagine the 'cure' is worse than the bite and is not recommended.

Many birds, however, seem to eat the berries without ill effect and it is around these yew trees that I once again encountered the flocks of finches. The noise and number of birds became so great that at one point I started wondering whether I was in some macabre Alfred Hitchcock film.

Turn left along the road and on for 30 yards to a public footpath sign on the right for Slate Hill. Follow this downhill to the old buildings behind Halecat House. Continue on the track to the left for 50 yards before turning off to the right on a thin, indistinct path through the grass where you see a summer house. This leads through an old orchard to another track. Turn right and up to the junction of tracks outside Halecat House and gardens. Here is a chance to relax and admire the gardens of this ancient house.

Halecat House was built around 1846 by Mr.J. Wanklyn for the 14th Earl of Derby. The Stanleys had held this title since the Battle of Bosworth when Thomas Stanley's support for Henry VII and the Lancastrians earned him the title of first Earl. In addition he was granted land throughout Lancashire and here in Witherslack. Choosing to live at Knowsley, near Liverpool, it wasn't until the 14th Earl came along that the Stanleys began to live in this region on a regular basis. The 14th Earl had two sons. The eldest inherited Knowsley and the younger was given the choice of an estate in Ireland or in Witherslack. Of course, he chose Witherslack and a Stanley has lived in the house ever since.

The present owners have done wonders with the gardens and grounds and are proud to show them off. The gardens are open to the public every day except Saturdays and Sunday mornings and admission is free. The impressively arranged beds and hedges include such acid loving plants as azaleas; no mean achievement on this limestone based soil. There is also a small gazebo complete with 300 – 500 year old stained glass, worth a visit in itself. The gardens are pleasant to stroll around and there should be time enough to do just that. There is even a nursery selling the offsprings from the garden, but you will have to carry them home.

After looking around the gardens and nursery retrace your steps along the track you came up. After 30 yards the wall around the nursery on your right comes to a corner. Here turn right along a track into the woods behind the nursery. Follow the track through a gap in the wall and on to a crossroads of paths. Here take the path straight ahead which leads through the woods and downhill to a gap in an old wall.

The woods around you are the perfect example of the hazel coppice and oak standard which was once, and still is, such a feature of this area. Coppicing woods has been a way of managing woodlands from the middle ages and virtually all the woods in Britain were once managed in this way. Originally most of the trees in the wood would be cut down just above ground level leaving the shoots to grow back from the stump. After 15 years or so the long, narrow 'poles' which had grown would be cut again and used for weaving fences, walls for houses and other light construction work. The most common tree used for coppicing was the hazel since this also provided an ample crop of nuts. In between the hazel coppices the woodsman would leave several oaks to reach maturity. These standards, as they were called, were used for larger beams and timber.

When man learnt how to smelt iron using charcoal, wood was in demand and coppicing was used to provide the wood needed for charcoal. During the summer and autumn the charcoal burner would live in the woods with his family. The wood was burnt in a shallow pit covered with sods and bracken allowing as little air as possible into the pit. This was how charcoal was formed. Charcoal for iron production is just one of the industries coppiced woods were used for. Later on we shall pass the remains of two other large users of the wood.

Go through the gap onto a clear track. Turn right and follow the track to a junction with a tarmac lane. Here continue straight ahead on the lane for three quarters of a mile as it curves in a large loop to the left.

You are now in the Winster Valley. The ancient boundary of Westmorland and Lancashire, this small, isolated valley was once under threat of flooding when Manchester Corporation were looking for extra water supplies. Manchester had already built Thirlmere and Haweswater to quench their thirst but in the 1960s they wanted more and went in search of another valley to flood. Winster was it, but the locals fought back and the Winster Protection Society saved the day. Mind you, some locals had little to say in favour of the valley and Lakes' author Norman Nicholson wrote "In almost every respect, except ugliness, it is a reservoir already. All that is needed is a dam.". Mind you, this is the same man who says of this valley "This is not walker's country.".

Eventually the tarmac lane becomes a track and soon after, a fork appears. Take the right fork, signed Wilson House, through the woods. Continue to the farm and then turn left through the wooden gate into the field. Follow the wall on your left to a metal footbridge. Cross this (into Old Lancashire!) and turn left to follow the river to the first field boundary. From here head for the diagonally opposite corner of the field and a gate. Go through this and follow the old hedge on your right to a metal gate at the far end. Turn right through the gate and along the path between the fences into the next field. Now follow the fence on your right until it leads off to the right. Here continue straight across the field following the power lines and yellow arrows to a pylon on the far side of the field. Behind the pylon is a gate and a tarmac track. Follow this, around the sheep pens, and on for 200 yards to a lane. Turn left on the lane which passes under the A590 and on towards Lindale. At the fork turn left down to the main street of Lindale.

The village of Lindale built on the slopes of Hampsfell and Newton Fell boasts two excellent public houses at either end of the main street. I'm sure it won't take much encouragement from me to enter either of these two hostelries before climbing Hampsfell. However, should you need an excuse then take a break to read about John Wilkinson, the local hero.

Off you go then!

Section 3: Lindale to Cartmel

Are you ready? Okay, I'll begin. John Wilkinson was the local boy made good. Born in 1728, his father, Issac, was a local iron maker who had a small furnace and forge at Wilson House near Lindale at a time when the whole of this area was an important iron producing centre. His father experimented using peat dug from the Winster Valley instead of charcoal, which may have helped his son with his future success. As John grew up the main fuel for iron smelting changed to coke and he went on to set up the first coke-powered blast furnace in the Black Country, in 1757. Things went from strength to strength and having married twice he used the money from these to further his success. He had always experimented with iron, building and floating iron boats in Helsington Pool as a boy. He went on to build real size iron boats as well as iron bridges, iron tombstones and he even invented the box type smoothing iron. One of his greatest successes was improvement in arms production, particularly in cannons and large guns. His success was tarnished slightly when he was involved in something of a scandal for selling a super gun to the French. This 'super gun' in fact turned out to be iron pipes for a new sewerage system.

John Wilkinson expanded more and more in the iron industry and became a prominent citizen of the time. As a man he was headstrong and proud and even had his own money minted to pay his workers, with a profile of himself on one side. He never forgot his roots though and bought Castlehead, a nearby rock promontory, on which he built his estate. In order to do this he transported tonnes of soil on horseback to the top of Castlehead and built a large garden on the previously bare rock. When he died in 1808 his will dictated he should be placed in a cast iron coffin and buried under an iron obelisk on Castlehead. Unfortunately, he did not die at Castlehead and crossing Morecambe Bay in its heavy, cast iron coffin, his body was almost lost for ever in the sand. The obelisk and coffin remained on Castlehead for 20 years until the estate changed hands. The new owners disliked the monument and had it removed and the coffin taken to Lindale church. The obelisk now stands in Lindale village, near the junction of the main street with the road for Grange, and his body can now, hopefully, rest in peace.

Walk up the main street of Lindale, past the Post Office to the first road on the left. Turn left along this road and follow it uphill past the school

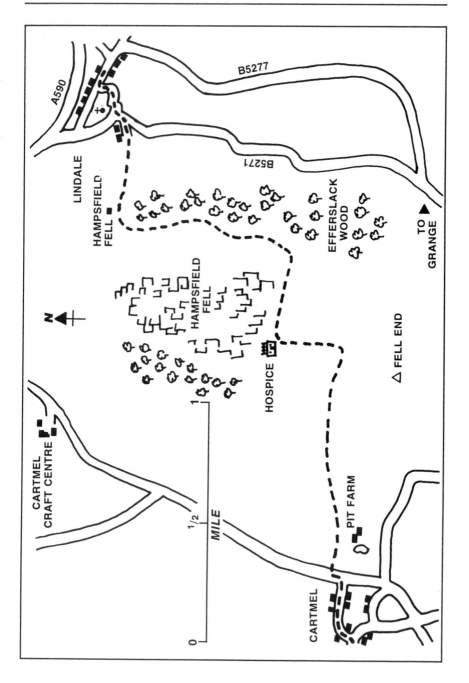

sign, then round to the left. Walk past the church to a T-junction. Turn left then quickly right up Lingarth. At the end of this road is a path and stone steps. Go up the steps into the field and then uphill to the metal gate at the top. After a few minutes to admire the view, go through the kissing gate and cross the lane to follow the path opposite. This leads down through the woods and into a field. Here go straight ahead to the right hand corner of the field and a wooden kissing gate. After the gate continue on towards the farm. Follow the yellow arrows through the metal gate. Pass in front of the farm before turning left at the wooden signpost for Hampsfell. Walk along the track, through the gate and then by the wall on your left to a stone stile into the woods. Go over this and along the path through the woods to a narrow V-gap by a gate. Pass through this (breathe in!) and onto a track. Follow this track by the wall until it passes through a metal gate. Continue for another third of a mile to a metal sign for Hampsfell.

Hampsfell, across which you are currently walking, is a fine example of a limestone fell. The woods of oak on its eastern slopes are bounded by superbly built dry stone walls of giant limestone rocks. The western slopes of the fell are the grazing lands of the Cartmel farmers with typical limestone flowers in abundance. On the top is a limestone pavement, with its clints and grykes forming a giant path of stones sheltering damp loving plants in its dark crevices. Between the slabs of rock is a calcareous grassland dotted with harebells.

Turn right at the sign to follow the track uphill as it zig-zags to a stone stile in the wall. Go over this and turn right, following the yellow arrow to the corner of the wall. From here follow the little wooden sign with the monk carved on it (pointing out the Cistercian Way) straight ahead to the hospice on top of Hampsfell.

The top of Hampsfell is a wonderful viewpoint, with Morecambe Bay displayed before you, and the Hospice here is something of a local landmark. During the middle of the 17th century a local pastor, Mr. Remington, would climb Hampsfell from his house at Longlands, every morning before breakfast. So fond was he of the view from the fell that he decided to build a hospice here for the rest and shelter of any traveller. The result is this intriguing limestone hut which contains not only a small fireplace and stone seats but also careful instructions for users of the hospice as well as 'The Answers' (although what the

The Hospice on Hampsfell

questions are, is not clear). As well as venturing inside, be sure to climb the precarious stone steps at the side to the giant compass on the roof. Here you can spot your favourite fells (if the weather is clear enough) using the indicator. This compass was added, after the hospice was built, by a Mr. Garstang, a retired railway engineer.

The top of Hampsfell is also the scene of something which shames the name of Cartmel – 'The Hampsfield Fight'. During the Jacobite rebellion the village folk were afraid of invasion by the Scots and assembled on the top of the fell to defend themselves. All able men of Cartmel, armed with any weapons they had, were gathered and together they drew up a plan of action. They would send Harry Barwick on one of his fast horses, across the sands to find out the position of the Scots. He would report back to the 'army' who would then take action. So they sat and waited as Harry disappeared across the Bay. And they waited. And they waited. Eventually they spotted Harry riding like the wind back across the sands. Thinking he must be fleeing from the Scots the men of Cartmel took immediate action. They ran away! Off they went back to the safety of their houses and locked the doors. Poor Harry returned to find the whole village hiding from him and nobody prepared to let him in. "Cowards" he called to them, "I only went a short distance before riding back intending to scare you and test your mettle". Obviously their mettle was not up to scratch.

From the Hospice take the clear path south (if you are not sure which way is south, check with the giant compass) along the fell top. Pass over the stile after 200 yards, through the gap in the old wall and continue until you reach a fork in the path. Take the right fork, following the arrows, to a crossroads of paths. Turn right to follow the arrows and the clear path downhill to a metal kissing gate. Go through the gate, across the field by the wall to a metal signpost. Continue ahead to another metal signpost by a gate. Go through the gate and bear half left to the diagonally opposite corner of the field by the farm buildings. From here cross the track in front of the farm to a sign for Cartmel. Turn right to follow the sign across the field and out onto the road. Turn left then right down the road into Cartmel Village.

TOUR DAY 2: CARTMEL

Accommodation

Unlike Levens, Cartmel village is much more catered towards the tourist, although still far enough off the beaten track to remain largely unspoilt. As a result there are half a dozen or so guest houses in the village itself, all offering reasonable prices and comfortable accommodation. You should be able to turn up, knock on a door and find accommodation at almost any time of the year except during Cartmel Races. During this time, beds in Cartmel are like gold dust and you will need to book well

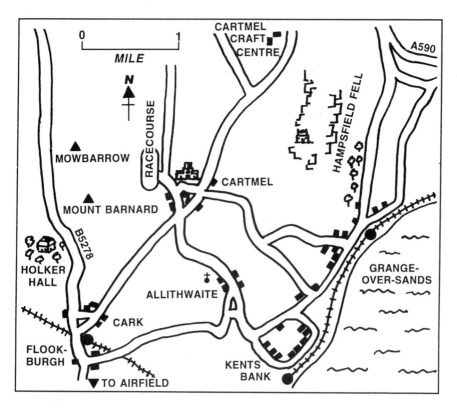

in advance. Even then you may find yourself having to spend the night in nearby Grange.

CARTMEL

Cartmel village, as villages go in this part of the world, is a fairly recent addition. The name Cartmel comes from *ceart* meaning rocky and rough and *melr* meaning a sand-bank. Hence a rocky sand-bank. The name, like the village and the area, is one of contrasts.

Originally Cartmel applied only to this wedge of land which pushes out into Morecambe Bay, resembling a mini-India. This parish of Cartmel, "with all the Britons in it", was once given by the King of Northumberland to the Bishop of Lindisfarne, St. Cuthbert in 670 AD. It remained in church hands up until the time of Henry VIII and the Dissolution. It was not until 1190, however, that the Priory of Cartmel

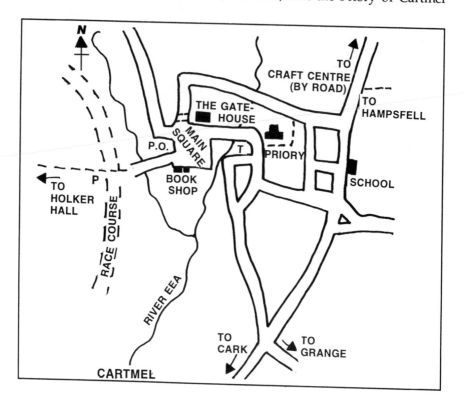

was built on the marshy land between the River Eea and Mere Beck. The village of Cartmel then built up around the Priory, but even up to the middle of the last century, it was still called 'Cartmel Churchtown'.

A window shopper in Cartmel's square

What of the village today? What is it like? Well, not that different from when it was first built. Edwin Waugh the writer sums up Cartmel when he says of it "like going to bed". It certainly has that nice cosiness about it which many other villages lack. Everything revolves around the main square, which itself is picture postcard stuff of ivy-clad and white-washed pubs and shops, together with great, grey stoned houses. The square has its own market cross, though no market, and a water-pump and stone trough for watering your horses at. Cartmel has many good shops including a particularly good second-hand book shop and a post office that sells sticky toffee pudding. If this makes you hungry then the village has many good places to eat, including several pubs in and around the square. It was into one of these that Edwin Waugh ventured in search of food. "I found hungry wood cutters sitting within" he relates, "waiting for a great dish of lobscouse prepared by a handsome, good natured landlady". I doubt you will find many wood cutters in the pubs today and you will be hard pressed to find lobscouse on the menu, but the landladies are still the same.

Cartmel really is a gem of a village which you can easily spend a whole day in if you take time to explore all its nooks and crannies, but not far away are many other delights to occupy your 'day-off'.

CARTMEL PRIORY

The Priory church in Cartmel really is the village's crowning glory. In many other small villages, such a large building could look ill-placed or uncomfortable but here in Cartmel it is totally at home. This great, grey slab of a building somehow only adds to the cosiness of the village.

A rare view of Cartmel Priory - from inside the walls!

The Priory's history goes back to 1185 when King John gave the whole of Cartmel to the Earl of Pembroke, William Marshall. He in turn founded a priory here in 1189, turning over the land, as well as other land in Ireland, to the Canons Regular of St. Augustine or the Black Canons as they were known. Initially the monks set up camp on a knoll just to the west of the present village. Here they had a vision from God who told them to build the new priory between two rivers, one flowing north and the other south. For many months they searched the whole of Cartmel, until one day, returning from another unsuccessful mission, one of the monks noticed that the two rivers which they crossed every day were flowing in opposite directions. The sacred place was under their noses all the time. So here they built the Priory from which the village of Cartmel grew. As a reminder of the vision they built a small chapel on the knoll, which became known as Mount Bernard. Though the chapel has long since gone the hill still retains the name.

The priory itself has undergone several changes during its history, the first of which was the addition of the Gatehouse, which still stands in the village square. This was added in 1340 to protect the monks from the raiding Scots and has since been used as a grammar school and a craftshop.

The order of monks at Cartmel were much less strict than their Cistercian neighbours in Furness and the local people were allowed to use the priory church for their own worship. It was this that saved the church from destruction during the Dissolution. In 1537 all the lands of Cartmel were taken from the Priory by the Crown and some of the canons were hanged. The Priory itself was due to be demolished but the locals stopped this happening by claiming the church was also a parish church used by the Cartmel people. The Crown relented. They did not demolish the church, merely stripped the lead from the roof and sold the church back to the villagers at an extortionate price. This left the Cartmellians extremely short of cash and they could not afford to repair the roof. The whole place was, unfortunately, left to rot. Then in 1618 George Preston of nearby Holker Hall, came to the rescue. He helped the parishioners raise the necessary money to re-roof the church, repair the general decay and even provided a magnificent carved oak screen and choir canopies. It is said that he imported the best Flemish carvers to do the job and at the same time got them to do some work on Holker Hall.

In 1643 the church was to suffer again when a detachment of Roundheads from the Civil War stayed in the church overnight. They stabled their horses in the church, destroyed the new organ and generally smashed up anything they took offence to. They even used the south-west door for target practice. The bullet holes can still be seen today as a reminder of those Cromwellian lager-louts. After this the church again went into decline until 1830 when a restoration programme lasting 40 years was started.

The Priory has changed little since then. From the outside it has a very square, squat look with its unusual tower within a tower resembling a tiered wedding cake. Inside, the architecture reflects its various stages through history with features from the Transitional, Decorated and Perpendicular periods. Even if you know nothing about architecture or history, the Priory is a wonderfully imposing building to explore. Some parts such as the great East Window and the carved oak screen are worth seeing in order to admire the craftsmen who created them. Also, look out for the peculiarities of the Priory such as the loaves of bread left by one of the columns. These are paid for by a bequest of one Rowland Briggs who died in 1703 and are to be "distributed to the most indigent of the parish every Sunday for ever.".

A special treat is the Priory's Open Day. On this one day in August there are special exhibitions, a chance to see many of the rare books held in the Priory, guided tours of the tower and even a chance to walk inside the walls through the narrow gaps which run throughout the structure. However, you will have to plan carefully since they only hold the open day every two years!

Opening Times: The Priory is open to the public every day of the year from 9.00 a.m. to 3.30 p.m. in winter and 5.30 p.m. in summer, though obviously it is still used for services on Sunday mornings and various other times.

The Priory Gatehouse is owned by the National Trust and is open to the public from April to November on Tuesdays to Sundays from 11.00 a.m. to 5.00 p.m. If the Gatehouse is shut during these times, it is because the keyholder has just popped home. It can be opened by ringing him on Cartmel (05395) 36691.

Admission: Admission for both the Priory and the Gatehouse is free, although the Priory welcomes voluntary contributions towards the upkeep of this important church.

HOLKER HALL

Holker Hall lies $1^1/_2$ miles to the south of Cartmel and holds many delights for lovers of houses and gardens. First of all you need to pronounce it correctly. The proper way is Hooker Hall. Next, a little of its history. The original Hall was built in the 16th century for the Preston family. The Prestons were great benefactors of the area and it was George Preston who did so much for Cartmel Priory. Indeed the family tomb can still be seen in the Priory's north wall.

The house was later altered in 1840 when it passed to the Cavendish family. In 1871 the house suffered a terrible fire, destroying much of the building. Using wood from the extensive estate and local stone throughout, the Cavendishes had the Hall rebuilt by Paley and Austin, the most famous northern architects of the time. The result is a fine example of a mock Elizabethan building which is grand and imposing on the outside and light and airy on the inside. Today the present Lord and Lady Cavendish live in the old wing of the house, the remains of the original Hall. The new wing as built by Paley and Austin is opened to the public and is rare in stately homes in not having ropes or barriers to restrict your movements through the rooms.

The Hall is famous for its detailed interior wood carving in many of the rooms as well as its distinctive furniture and paintings. The library alone contains some 3,500 books and what the owners describe as 'an amusing secret'. You will have to visit the Hall yourself to find out what this is!

Outside, there is still more to see. The 22 acres of Gardens were originally set out by the 7th Duke of Devonshire, the same Lord Cavendish who rebuilt the Hall after the fire. Described as 'amongst the best gardens in the world' by the Good Garden Guide, they contain a mixture of truly impressive formal gardens, sprawling bluebell woodland and beautifully simple water features such as a splashing limestone cascade. The grounds also hold the oldest Chilian Pine (monkey puzzle tree) in the country and a new attraction is the wildflower meadow, specially managed to encourage the growth of native grassland flowers. The estate extends outside of the Gardens for another 120 acres or so and in recent times has been turned into a deer park containing one of the oldest herds of fallow deer in England.

If old houses or gardens are not your style then Holker Hall has more to tempt you. The Hall is home to the Lakeland Motor Museum, a private collection of over 80 vintage cars, cycles and other automobilia. There is a reproduction garage from the 1920s together with a motorist's shop and Esso exhibition. This is a real must for any car fanatic.

If you want more, then Holker supplies it. There is an exhibition of antique household appliances which reconstructs kitchens from Victorian, Edwardian and wartime periods. (Be prepared to say 'I had one of those' or 'My mother had one like that'). There is also a patchwork and quilting shop, showing and selling a wide variety of patchwork quilt covers and other goods. This includes a workshop in patchworking every Tuesday. Those interested need to pre-book their place by ringing (05395) 58021. If you still have time to spare then there is a craft and countryside exhibition, guided discovery walks and adventure playgrounds for the younger visitors.

Holker Hall with all its attractions could easily fill a whole day, although a visit to the House, Garden and Motor Museum does work out fairly expensive. You can take your own packed lunch and many people are to be found by the picnic tables, but there is also a self-service cafeteria.

In addition to the usual attractions, the Hall also holds several annual events which you could coincide with your visit and make a real day of it. Though the events change each year, the regular ones include the Barbour Horse Trial, a three day event of dressage, cross-country and show jumping, which attracts all the top riders. This occurs at the end of July. There is also a hot air balloon rally in September with a mass display of 20 to 30 balloons, a rally of MG cars in August and the Great Garden and Countryside Festival in June. For details of any of these events or for information on the Hall in general, ring (05395) 58328.

Getting There: It is possible to catch a bus from Cartmel to Cark, a few hundred yards from the Hall entrance, but these are not particularly frequent. The easiest and most pleasant way to Holker is to walk the $1^1/_2$ miles across the fields on a clear track.

From the main square in Cartmel take the small lane on the left of the post office, which leads into the car park by the race course. Continue straight across the car park and through the wooden gate at the far end. Follow the track straight ahead, across the race track and through the gate on the other side. Continue on the track to another gate sporting a 'Beware of adders' sign. Go through the gate, watching out for snakes, and continue on the track as it leads through the woods. At the fork in the track, just after the woods clear, take the right fork. This later becomes a tarmac lane leading to a gate and public footpath sign. Here turn off the tarmac lane through the gate with another 'Beware of adders' sign, into the woods. Follow the clear bridleway through the woods to a road. Turn left on the road, taking care since there is no footpath at first, and continue for 500 yards to the entrance to Holker Hall on the right.

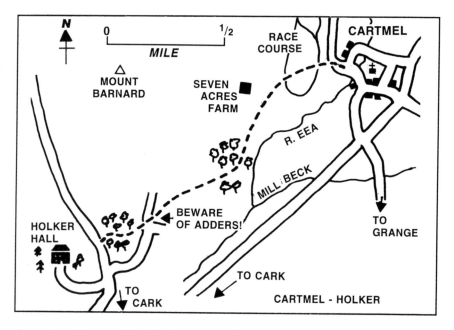

Opening Times: The Hall is open from April to October every day except Saturdays. The gates open at 10.30 a.m. and close at 6.00 p.m. with the last admission at 4.30 p.m.

Admission: On entrance to the grounds you will be given several choices of ticket depending on what you want to visit. The cheapest is for the Gardens and grounds only and is reasonably cheap (band A). The next most expensive provides entrance to the Gardens and House or

Gardens and Motor Museum (band B) and the most expensive provides entry to all three (band B). All the other exhibitions such as the Zanussi collection of household appliances are free on all the tickets.

During the annual events you will have to pay more depending on the event. You should ring beforehand for more information.

CARTMEL CRAFT CENTRE

Have you ever fancied trying your hand at oil painting? Is there a frustrated artist in you, trying to get out? What about water-colours? Do you fancy yourself as the next Turner? If so, then Cartmel Craft Centre may be for you. The Craft Centre, based in old farm buildings north of Cartmel, runs various art courses throughout most of the year. These cover a wide range of subjects from landscapes to detailed flower portraits in either oils or water-colours. Whether you are a beginner or an experienced artist, you can pick up techniques and tips from the Centre's resident artist. The courses run all day with a break for lunch and all materials can be supplied at an extra cost.

If painting on canvas or paper is not your cup of tea then the Centre also runs courses on fabric decoration, dried flower arrangement and calligraphy. These also last all day, apart from the calligraphy which are run on various afternoons. The courses are spread out over various Wednesdays, Thursdays and Fridays between May and October and you should check the dates with the Centre beforehand. If there is not a course running on the right day for you then individual tuition can be arranged on an hourly rate.

For your lunch hour the Centre contains the Egg-Pudding Stone Restaurant. This is a licensed restaurant – should you wish to find artistic inspiration in a bottle – which sells good, whole-food dishes, including some wicked puddings! The restaurant is open to all visitors, not just course members, since the Centre also contains a display of workshops where you can watch traditional craftsmen at work, a studio and gallery of local artists and a shop selling various hand-made items. There is much to see for everyone interested in crafts at the Centre, although if you are not taking one of the courses, it would only occupy a couple of hours. For more information on courses or tuition ring Cartmel (05395) 36009.

Getting There: The only convenient way to get to the Centre is to walk. There are two ways to the Centre on foot; one is straight up the road from Cartmel, which is $1^1/2$ miles and the other is the more scenic route along Hampsfell which extends the walk to $2^1/2$ miles. The choice is yours.

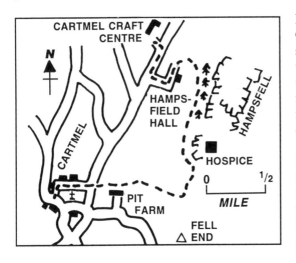

From the square in Cartmel, retrace your steps from the main walk, past the back of the Priory to the main road. Here turn left and if taking the short way, continue walking for $1^1/2$ miles to Broughton Lodge Farm and Cartmel Craft Centre. Otherwise walk for just 50 yards to the signpost on the right for Hampsfell and the path you followed yesterday. Follow the path back across the field, then uphill before turning left at the top of the hill to make your way back to the Hospice.

Some 50 yards before the Hospice, take a small path to the left which leads around the rock outcrop on which the Hospice stands. Continue on the path as it leads past the Hospice above you, and on for a quarter of a mile to a gate and stone stile in a wall. Go over the stile and follow the path through the Scots pines. Continue on the path which follows the edge of the woods, along the ridge of Hampsfell.

Strolling along the path offers, not only excellent views up the Winster Valley, but some interesting features under your feet. This limestone ridge supports many small, but beautiful flowers and two of the most common here are wild thyme and eyebright. You should also notice the occasional small hump of ground, sprouting up from the grass. If you look carefully at these humps you will see that they are made of tiny particles of soil covered by a dense mat of wild thyme binding them all together. These are in fact ant hills and are a common feature of calcareous grasslands. They are made by yellow or meadow ants which use the hill for protection, storing food, rearing the brood and farming aphids. The ants need some sort of sugary fluid for energy and obtain this from honeydew which is a waste product of the sap-sucking aphids. The yellow ants tend to farm root aphids in much the same way as humans farm cows for milk.

The hills themselves are made by worker ants continually piling soil particles on the top of the hill and because of this they have an ecology of their own. Rosette plants such as daisies or cowslips cannot tolerate ants dropping soil on them all the time, so the only plants which grow on the mound are creeping plants such as wild thyme. Inside the hill, the temperature rises as the sun shines on it. As the sun moves around the sky, the ants move the brood of cocoons to the warmest part. If you get a small twig and gently scrape away a few pieces of soil, you will probably spot the ants crawling around and may even see a few carrying a white cocoon. Please do not disturb them too much though. After all, it is their home.

Eventually the path leads downhill at the end of the ridge to a wooden gate in the bottom left hand corner of the field. Go through this gate into a field and follow the woodland edge on your left, to a metal gate. After the gate follow the arrow straight across the field to a gate opposite, onto a track. Turn left and follow the track to and into a farmyard. Turn right along the farm track to the road. Turn right again and along the road for a quarter of a mile to Broughton Lodge Farm and Cartmel Craft Centre.

Opening Times: The Centre is open from Easter to October, though courses only run from May. The Centre does not open Mondays and Tuesdays and arranged courses run Wednesdays to Fridays. It is possible to arrange individual tuition when courses are not being held.

The Centre opens at 11.00 a.m. and closes at 5.00 p.m. Courses usually run from 11.00 a.m. to 4.00 p.m. with an hour for lunch.

Admission: Admission to the Centre is free. Courses are reasonably expensive (bands D to F) though for a full day's tuition are on a par with normal evening classes. Materials for the art courses can be supplied if required at a small additional cost. Materials for other courses are included in the price. Individual tuition, paid for by the hour, is more expensive but you do get individual attention.

GRANGE-OVER-SANDS

Grange-over-Sands, described as the Torbay of the North or the Riviera of Cumbria, does tend to catch the sun and have higher spring temperatures than the rest of the area, but it is a little more Darby and Jones than Bridget Bardot. If a day by the seaside is what you want though, then look no further than Grange.

Grange or St. Tropez?

Grange-over-Sands gets its name from its origin as a grain store for the local monks. Besides the grange, the monks also had a vineyard (I said it was warm!) and a small harbour, transporting goods to and from their lands in Ireland. It was also the home of the 'sands guide' which the Priory was obliged to keep to guide travellers across the treacherous sands of Morecambe Bay. This is how Grange-over-Sands gets its curious name, since to get to Cartmel from Lancaster you would walk or ride to Grange-over-the-sands.

After the Dissolution of the Priory, Grange fell into decline becoming a small fishing hamlet. The sand guide was too important to lose, however, so a guide was maintained by the Duchy of Lancaster and given his own house at Guides Farm to the south of the town. Here the current guide, Cedric Robinson, still lives, guiding parties across the sands. If you fancy a walk across Morecambe Bay sands then talk to Mr Robinson on Grange (05395) 2165. Never, ever attempt crossing the sands without a guide. It has infamously dangerous quicksand and any reader of this book is far too valuable to lose!

Grange, meanwhile, remained a small village of around 260 people until the coming of the railway in 1857. The railway brought tourists and Grange's moderate temperatures and undoubted beauty made it a popular seaside town of Victorian times. Several large hotels were built, including the Crown and the Grange, both of which can still be seen along the seafront. In 1904 the promenade was built and this pleasant walk by the sea is still one of Grange's most attractive features. The healing waters of Holy Well at nearby Humphrey Head, made the resort even more fashionable. They were once famed as a remedy for "stones, gout and cutaneous complaints".

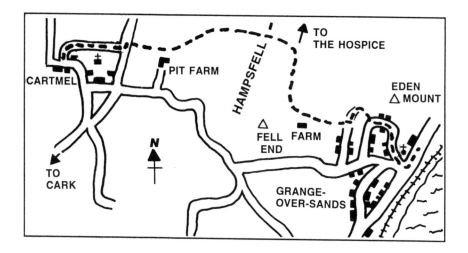

Today the resort remains much the same as it was during its Victorian heyday. It even seems as though the people are the same sometimes, since Grange is a popular retirement town (perhaps it should be known as the Eastbourne of the North). The town does hold many other attractions though. For instance, the town's front, although separated from the sea by the railway line, is a pleasant mixture of shops and ornamental gardens which make interesting viewing. There are also tennis courts, a putting green, bowling greens and for the brave hearted, an open air swimming pool. For a quiet, relaxing day by the sea there is nowhere better. Besides, my mum likes it – so it can't be bad.

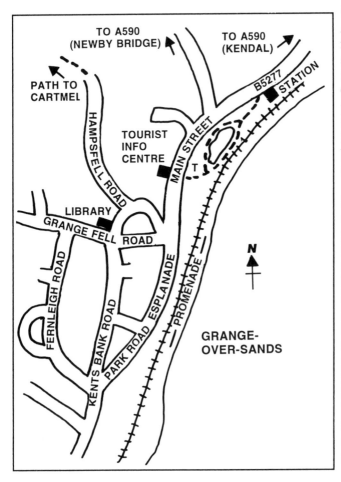

Getting There: Again, the local, infrequent bus service does run from Cartmel to Grange, but a pleasant 2 mile stroll over Hampsfell is the best way to enter the town.

From Cartmel square, retrace your steps from the main walk along the street behind the Priory to the main road. Turn left along the road for 50 yards to the sign for Hampsfell on the right. Turn right and follow the path across the fields and uphill to the crossroads of paths on the top of the ridge. Here continue straight ahead and then right on a clear path heading downhill through the bracken. Follow this to a metal gate and stile. Go over the stile and take the path to the left, past an old wall to a wooden gate onto a tarmac lane. Cross the lane and follow the sign for Ashurst Road through the gap in the wall. Head towards the left of the house to a metal gate onto the lane. Continue downhill on the lane into the farmyard.

As you enter the farmyard you will see a stone stile in the wall on your left. Go over this and cross the field by the wall on your right hand side to a stone stile opposite. After the stile follow the path by the walled garden to the road by the houses (Ashurst Gardens). Turn left to the end of this cul-de-sac. Here you will find a small path which leads onto a track. Turn right on the track and follow it to Hampsfell Road. Turn left and follow the road downhill into the centre of Grange-over-Sands.

CARTMEL RACES

If you should be lucky enough to find yourself in Cartmel during May or August Bank Holiday weekends, you will be amazed by the traffic, the hustle and the sheer number of people milling through the small village. For it is during these two weekends of the year that the Cartmel steeplechase takes place and the village really comes to life. Cartmel racecourse lies at the back of the village, squashed between woodland and houses, making it the smallest and probably most attractive race course in the country. Visit it on any normal day and the flat, empty course, denude of its fences looks like some great, lawn covered drive to a non-existent stately pile. Visit it on raceday and you see it as it should be. The centre of the course, usually an empty playing field, is covered by marquees, stalls and the caravans of the fairfolk who set up a small fairground here. The course itself now has its brush fences erected and there are bookies everywhere.

The atmosphere is wonderful, with a real carnival feeling and it is not surprising that these National Hunt meetings attract all the big names. If you have wanted to go racing, forget Ascot with all its finery, forget Aintree and the Grand National, Cartmel is a real close-up, hands on steeplechase where you can almost smell the horses' breath as they thunder past.

Opening Times: Cartmel Steeplechases occur twice a year at Spring and late Summer Bank Holidays. Racing takes place on Saturdays and Mondays with a day off on Sundays.

Admission: Admission ranges in price depending on whether you wish to stand or sit (band B to C). This gets you in for the whole day and once in the ground there are the refreshment tents, stalls and fairground. For more information ring Witherslack (044 852) 228.

FLOOKBURGH STEAM GATHERING

Flookburgh is a small ex-market town, 2 miles to the south of Cartmel. Famous for its fluke fishing, Flookburgh has another great attraction. Once a year people from all over the country and abroad, gather to view the large display of steam powered engines which meet on Flookbourgh airfield. The Gathering must surely be one of the largest in the country and for any steam enthusiast, a day in heaven. There are traction engines, authentic steam rollers, steam tractors and any other steam vehicle you can mention. There are also many other vintage cars and lorries, all in working order and on display. For anyone who enjoys the sound of a whistle or the sight of powerful monsters gleaming and shining, this is a memorable day out.

Getting There: Although the town of Flookburgh is reachable by bus, the airfield lies another mile to the south of the town and not on any bus route. You could walk it, but it would be along a tarmac lane busy with cars heading for the Gathering. The easiest way to get there is probably by taxi either from Cartmel or Flookburgh. This, of course, adds to the expense.

Opening Times: The Gathering occurs just one weekend in July. Check with the local Tourist Information Centre at Grange on (05395) 34026 to find out the exact dates.

Admission: Entrance prices are reasonable (band B) and there is much to see and do once inside.

WALK DAY 3:
CARTMEL TO NEWBY BRIDGE

Route: Cartmel – How Barrow – Grassgarth – Bigland Tarn – Low Wood – Backbarrow – Newby Bridge.

Distance: $7^1/_2$ miles.

Maps: 1:50,000 O.S. Landranger No. 97 Kendal to Morecambe or 1:25,000 O.S. Pathfinder No. 636 Grange-over-Sands and 1:25,000 O.S. Pathfinder No. 626 Broughton-in-Furness

Getting There: Cartmel, and the start of today's walk, lies at the heart of the Cartmel peninsular amongst a mass of small lanes that criss-cross the area. There is no quick way by car and it is a case of following the A590 from the M6 until you see the clear signs for Cartmel pointing to the left. Follow any of these to the village.

The village is notoriously difficult to get to by public transport. There are buses – notably the 530/1 from Kendal to Ulverston – but these are infrequent, especially during school holidays. The nearest train station is at Grange-over-Sands two miles to the south and the buses from Kendal also join Grange to Cartmel. In some ways it would be easier and more pleasant, if just doing the day's walk as a one-off, to start the walk from Grange, walking over Hampsfell to Cartmel (see last chapter for directions).

The Walk

This is the shortest walk of the whole Trail, but there is much to occupy us on the way. From Cartmel, we start with a gradual climb up to How Barrow Fell which offers some of the best views across Morecambe Bay – not just across the Kent Sands to Lancashire but the other way towards Furness over Cartmel Sands. From here the walk contours along the side contours along the side of the ridge to Bigland Tarn before plunging downhill through coppiced woods to the hamlet of Low Wood. Here there is plenty of time to look around the old Clock Tower and admire the glass engraving at Artcrystal before strolling along the River Leven to Backbarrow. A short stride across the fells from here brings you to Newby Bridge at the end of Windermere.

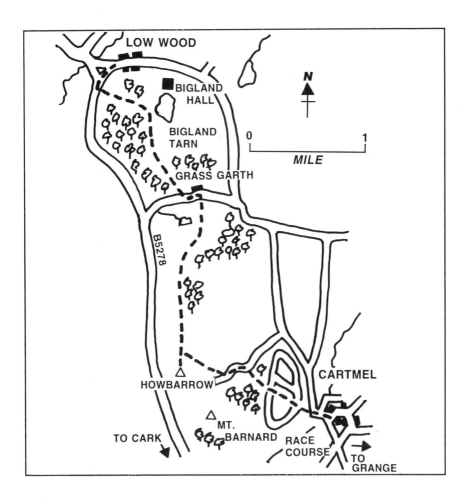

Section 1: Cartmel to Low Wood

From the square in Cartmel village take the small lane to the left of the post office which leads to the car park by the race course. As you enter the car park turn right to follow the public footpath sign across the middle of the race course, bearing right towards a gate in the wall into the woods. Pass through this gate and follow the path uphill through the woods and out through the narrow slit at the top. Now follow the clear path across the field to a stile onto the lane. Turn left on the lane and follow it for half a mile to a fork in the lane. Take the left fork towards Yew Barrow Farm and on for 100 yards to Howbarrow Farm.

As you walk along the tarmac lane you will not fail to see a small wooded hill on your left. This is Mount Barnard where the monks at Cartmel had their angelic vision.

At the farm turn right and follow the track uphill to a gate. Go through the gate and turn right along a track which leads by the wall. Continue uphill to a gateway in the wall. From here turn left up to the top of How Barrow, a few yards away, to admire the view.

From here you can take in Morecambe Bay in all its desolate splendour. If the tide is out it appears as a long stretch of sand – a barren desert of mudflats and pools. Away to the east you can see the coast of Lancashire quite clearly stretching southwards. To the west, separated by another stretch of sand, is the Furness peninsular with the monstrous, grey block of the Glaxo factory clearly visible. From this point it is clear why the Cartmel peninsular became an important crossing point when the main highway into south Lakeland was across the sand.

The route across the sands has been used since Roman times when the Roman generals marched their legions across. During the raids of 1322 Robert the Bruce led the Scots across Cartmel Sands to burn and pillage the farms of Cartmel. Because of the marshes of the Lyth Valley the sands were, until the building of the turnpike road and causeway in 1820, the safest and quickest way into Furness. For one or two hours each day the sands were alive with traffic. The crossing was not without its dangers though and parish registers record the unlucky souls lost in quicksand or swept away by the currents. For this reason there has always been a guide, or rather two guides, for travellers. The guide based at Kents Bank is the best known and was originally funded by the Priory at Cartmel. He would guide travellers across Kent Sands from Arnside or Hest Bank to Kents Bank. After spending the night in Cartmel, the traveller would then cross to Furness over Cartmel Sands under the care of the second guide, funded by Conishead Priory. Both these guides still exist though now receive their meagre payment from a charitable trust.

Even the turnpike road did not kill off the sands as a major highway and up until the middle of the 1800s there was a regular coach service from Ulverston to Lancaster across the sands. It was the coming of the railway that sent the route into decline. You can see the great sweep of the railway track as it crosses the Leven estuary on one side and loops around the peninsula to cross the Kent on the other side. The crossing of the sands has now been reduced to the guide leading groups of up to 500 people at a time across the Bay to raise money for charity.

From the top of How Barrow return through the gateway in the wall and turn left to follow the track northwards with the wall on your left hand side. Follow the track for quarter of a mile to a gate in the wall. After the gate go straight ahead to a corner of a wall and a fence. Follow the path ahead with the wall on your right hand side to a metal gate. Go through the gate and bear slightly right onto a clear track which passes through a gateway. Continue straight ahead following the wall on your right hand side for half a mile to another metal gate.

Walking along this ridge with the estuary of the River Leven below you, you may have noticed the different landscape of this rocky ridge compared to Hampsfell across the valley. The ground here is much more gnarled than the smoother limestone outcrop of Hampsfell and the fields don't display as many bright flowers. There is a reason for this and its all down to rocks. The rock under Hampsfell is limestone, something of a conspicuous feature of this walk so far. The rock under How Barrow and the rest of this ridge is an extension of the Silurian slates which surround Windermere. The meeting point of the two rocks is the Eea Valley running through the heart of Cartmel.

Go through the gate and follow the path ahead uphill, parallel with the wall on your left, until you reach a metal gate in this wall. Pass through this and turn right through a metal gate in a wire fence. From here bear half left around the rocky outcrop before heading downhill towards the white house of Grassgarth. At the bottom of the hill go through the gate onto the lane. Turn right along the lane for 75 yards to a public footpath sign for Low Wood. Turn left to follow the sign up the track to the house, where chickens and dogs run freely across your path. Follow the sign by the house through the field to the woods. Pass through the gate and up the clear track through Striber Woods. At the top of the hill you come out of the woods onto a clear track. Follow this as it bears to the left and past the yellow arrows to the tarn.

This is Bigland Tarn and the surrounding hills are Bigland Heights. It was across these Heights that a Mr. Robinson came walking one winter's day back in 1799. He was on his way to Broughton-in-Furness, but never made it since he came upon a poor, helpless beggar in the snow. He returned with the beggar to Cartmel. There he passed him on to the overseer who refreshed the beggar with tea and gin and called the doctor. The beggar, William Fearns, bemoaned his poverty and his condition but would allow no one to remove his wet and dirty clothes. It's not surprising then, that he caught a fever and died several days later. On removing his clothes he was found to have 185 guineas hidden in his trousers (a small fortune in those days) together with a false kidney stone and medical certificate which he had used to obtain money. A search for his relatives was made but none were found. The money was used to buy four fields near Grange and the revenue from these has been divided out to the local poor ever since.

Walk around the left-hand side of the tarn to the three-fingered signpost. Here follow the sign left for Low Wood. Bigland Tarn will probably have several fishermen dotted along its shores. The Tarn belongs to the estate of Bigland Hall which is open to the public and offers, in the best tradition of country sports, huntin', shootin' and fishin' as well as less bloodthirsty pursuits.

Follow the white arrows downhill by the wall on your right to a wooden gate into the trees. Go through the gate and follow the path downhill through the woods. After quarter of a mile the path comes to a glade where it splits. Here take the narrow path on the right as it continues downhill through the woods to the road (B5278). Turn right along the road for 50 yards before turning right again along a quieter lane. Follow this lane to the junction at Low Wood village. Here turn right then left down the short track to the Clock Tower and Artcrystal Studio.

Section 2: Low Wood to Newby Bridge

The Clock Tower buildings of Low Wood are an unmistakable landmark, a great, grey slate building with an imposing square column clock tower. The buildings now house a couple of businesses – an electrical goods shop and a crystal engravers – but they date back to 1849 when they formed the centre of the local gunpowder industry.

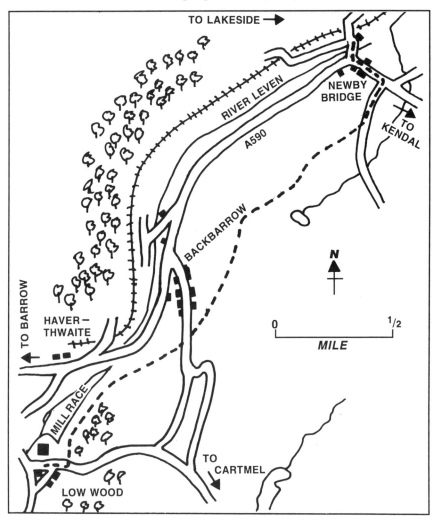

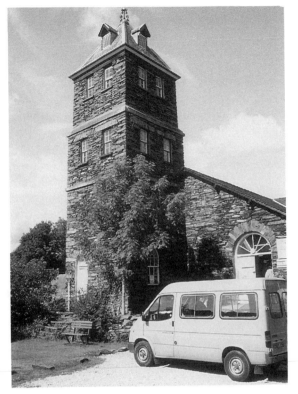

Low Wood Clock Tower

During the 18th century the use of charcoal for iron smelting was on the decline. The invention of the blast furnace and the use of coke meant that the charcoal burners of south Lakeland had a lack of demand for their product. So, like any good businessmen, they found new markets and gunpowder mills shot up all over Cumbria. The first mill opened in Sedgewick in 1764. Low Wood opened in 1798. Using charcoal from the local woods, together with saltpetre and sulphur imported up the River Leven, the mill soon became a thriving industry. It produced 'Africa' powder for ships, blasting powder for industry and 'country' powder for sport shooting. The powder was produced by grinding the three ingredients together under heavy stone rollers to form an intimate mixture. This was then pressed into hard sheets before being broken up, graded and glazed. Although every precaution was taken to avoid accidents, such as keeping the powder damp, the process was extremely dangerous and the history of Low Wood is littered with explosions and the death of workers.

The industry here at Low Wood underwent various mergers and extensions before finally closing in 1935. Many of the buildings were demolished for safety reasons and the few that remain are mainly on private land. However, here we can admire the impressive Clock Tower buildings which once housed the offices of the works together with the saltpetre and charcoal refineries. Opposite the Clock Tower is a small row of houses which were once the stable blocks. Low Wood is one of the best preserved gunpowder works in the country.

Today the Clock Tower buildings hold different and less hazardous enterprises. The first building holds an Aladdin's cave of reconditioned and shop-soiled electrical goods. Its wide floor space is covered by a tightly packed array of fridges, freezers and washing machines. The Clock Tower itself contains a different Aladdin's cave – a collection of bric-a-brac, pottery, ornaments, toys, books and many other small items which are worth a browse through. Even if it is simply to bring back childhood memories when you discover an old Beano annual. Next door is the Artcrystal studios of Patrick and Marian McMahon who produce beautiful, hand-crafted glass engravings. Patrick's work has a reputation around the world and he has produced items for Presidents and Royalty alike. His engravings have a special, three-dimensional quality and you can watch Patrick at work in his studio. If you are feeling extravagant you can even commission your own piece of work from him.

The Electrical Store is open every day 10.00 a.m. to 4.00 p.m. and the Artcrystal Studio is open week days only from 10.00 a.m. to 5.00 p.m. throughout the year. Admission to both is free.

After taking time to visit the sights, let's continue the walk.

From in front of the buildings walk back to the lane and turn left to pass in front of the houses to the woods and a bridleway sign. Turn left to follow the sign on the clear bridleway through the woods. Continue along the bridleway for three quarters of a mile to a farm and a dirt track which leads to the road.

At the start of the bridleway you will be walking by the main mill race from the River Leven, which once powered the gunpowder mill. In the 1950s the old mill race was extended and used to power a hydro-electric plant which feeds into the national grid.

As you start to climb and come out of the woods, below you in the Leven Valley you will spot a large, white building surrounded by a grey complex of houses and flats. This is the Whitewater Hotel and timeshares which stand on the site of the large iron foundry, which was once the heart of Backbarrow. With the decline of the iron industry the site was used for the production of 'Dolly Blue – your mother's washday friend'! It is now the home of Lakeland's newest industry, a timeshare leisure complex for tourists.

Along this stretch the garlic smell of woodland ramsons is replaced by one of aniseed. This comes from the large, white umbrella flowered plants dotted along the path. This is sweet cicely, so called because its leaves have a sugary taste. In summer it produces long, dark brown fruits which have a strong aniseed smell when crushed. In medieval times the crushed seeds were used to give a gloss and fragrance to oak furniture. Today the plant can be used in cooking, mainly in salads, giving a sweet, myrrh like taste.

Turn left on the road for 30 yards before turning right to follow a wooden public footpath sign along a track. Follow the track past the house and through a metal gate. Continue on the track over a footbridge and through the woods. Carry on through the woods, following the wall on your left hand side for half a mile, past the first ladder stile on your left to the next ladder stile ahead. Go over this and follow the clear track through the bracken to a wooden gate and stone stile on the opposite side of the field. Go over the stile and follow the track downhill to the road. Turn left on the road and walk 350 yards to the junction with the main road (A590). Turn left into Newby Bridge

TOUR DAY 3:
NEWBY BRIDGE

NEWBY BRIDGE

Newby Bridge is not really a village as such. It consists of nothing more than a string of guest houses, hotels and a few houses along the main A590. It derives its name from the 5-arched bridge which spans the River Leven at this point. Built in the 16th century this ancient bridge, with its sharply pointed buttresses and low arches is the first crossing of the Leven as it pours out of Windermere and heads seaward. Just downstream from the bridge is a long, diagonal weir which controls the flow of water out of the lake. This can best be seen on the north side of the river where a couple of benches have been set up to view about the only viewable thing in Newby Bridge. Also on this side of the river is the Swan Hotel, a rather expensive place to stay although it is pleasant to simply buy a drink and sit out by the river here in the evening.

Is this the only view in Newby Bridge?

Lakeside, three quarters of a mile upstream, also has little to offer the sightseer and exists only as a landing point for the steamer. All in all, today's tour day offers little in the way of museums and churches and nothing for the historic house or garden lover. Instead today is an activity day, with steam trains, steam boats and outdoor pursuits – both traditional and modern – to fill your day.

Accommodation

The one thing Newby Bridge does have in abundance is places to stay. There are hotels and bed and breakfasts along this stretch of the A590 of every grade and price. You should be able to turn up and find a room

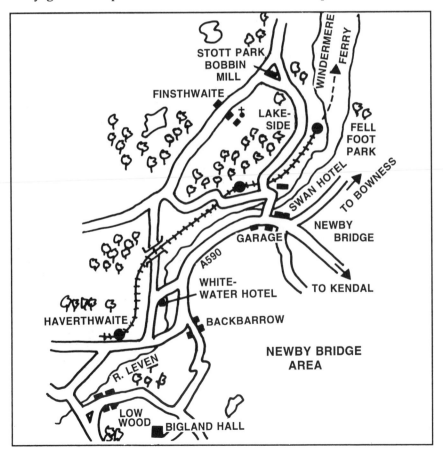

without much difficulty. There is no Tourist Information Centre here, the nearest being in Grange. So here are a few selected places of accommodation for those who like to book in advance.

Furness Fells, Newby Bridge. Tel. (05395) 31260
The Hollins B&B, Newby Bridge. Tel. (05395) 31383
The Swan Hotel, Newby Bridge. Tel. (05395) 31681

If you have problems finding a bed for the night, then Lakeside with another selection of hotels and guest houses is just three quarters of a mile up the road.

STOTT PARK BOBBIN MILL

The large blanket of woodland which covers much of this area has always been an important part of the local industry. Initially the wood was used to make charcoal to feed the iron industry then later on, to produce gunpowder. Stott Park Bobbin Mill represents the third major use for the local coppice crop. The wood gathered from coppiced trees had, for a long time, been used to make bobbins and spools. In fact the best poles were always used for this purpose, the rest being turned to

Stott Park Bobbin Mill

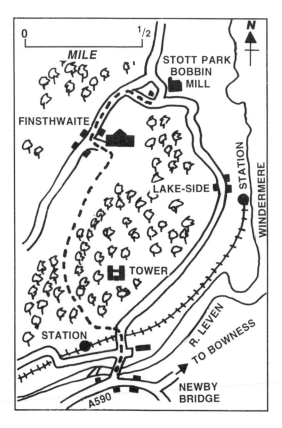

charcoal. Then, with the growth of the cotton and weaving industry in Lancashire in the 18th and 19th century, the demand for bobbins grew and bobbin making took on mass production proportions. Stott Park Bobbin Mill was built in 1835 and is a perfect example of many such mills which once covered Lakeland. The Mill today is preserved as a working museum and is little changed from nearly 160 years ago.

During its lifetime the Mill used its lathes, not only for the production of bobbins, but for many other wooden objects. Its product range included door knobs, hand grenade handles and duffle coat toggles for the Royal Navy. Although the Mill closed its commercial production in 1971 it is now preserved as an authentic display of 19th century machinery and working conditions. The only thing to have changed is that a new steam boiler now powers the tools and machinery rather than the water-wheel of old. For lovers of steam the boiler can be seen in action and there are guided tours of the Mill lasting 30-40 minutes.

Stott Park keeps the past alive and reminds us of yesterday's 'state of the art' equipment. It is set in beautiful woodland and worthy of a visit by anyone interested in wood, steam or just a pleasant day out. Although a visit to the Mill itself would not fill a whole day, combined with a visit to Finsthwaite Church and a stop off at Lakeside on the way back, making the rest of the journey by steam train, it would make a memorable day out.

Getting There: The only way to get to Stott Park from Newby Bridge is to walk. However, it is only a mile away, either up the road past Lakeside or on a much nicer stroll through the woods of Summer House Knott and Finsthwaite.

From the Swan Hotel at Newby Bridge take the road away from the river (signed for Lakeside) to pass over the railway bridge. After the bridge turn immediately left on a track into the woods. Follow this track (ignoring the sign on the right for Finsthwaite Tower) past the bungalow after 100 yards and up to a stile. Go over the stile and follow the path and yellow arrows uphill through the woods until you reach a stone stile in a wall. Go over the stile and into a field. Head straight across the field to an old wall and two stone pillars. Pass through the pillars and follow the yellow arrow across the next field to a ladder stile opposite. Cross the next field, over a stone stile and straight ahead to a gate on the left by Finsthwaite Church. Go through the gate onto a lane by the Church.

Finsthwaite's beautiful church

The Church at Finsthwaite is an odd looking structure with a squat, square tower centrally placed and an equally stubby steeple on top. It looks rather like a poor mismatch of two larger churches, but it does have a charm of its own which I am sure Finsthwaite parishioners would not swop for anything else. Inside, the Church has two original features; a wooden cross made from a plank of a pontoon bridge over the River Piave in Italy and a Communion cup made from an old gun shell. These were made at the end of World War One for the then vicar of Finsthwaite, who was an army padre during the war.

The Church graveyard also holds its own unique piece of history, the gravestone of Clementina Sobieska Douglas who died in 1771. Before she ended up here, Clementina lived at Waterside House in Newby Bridge and was said to be the daughter of a Scots lady, Clementina Walkinshaw and no less a person than Prince Charles Edward or Bonny Prince Charlie as he was popularly called. However, when the young Pretender found time to procreate on his visit to Kendal remains something of a mystery!

Turn left on the lane then take the right hand fork up to the road. Turn right and follow the road for 400 yards to the junction. Turn right, following the sign for the Bobbin Mill and the entrance for the Mill is 50 yards on, on the left.

Opening Times: The Mill is open from April to October, daily from 10.00 a.m. to 6.00 p.m.. The steam boiler is in operation on Tuesdays, Wednesdays and Thursdays – although it sometimes operates on additional days and it is worth checking beforehand. Tel. (05395) 31087.

Admission: Entrance prices are relatively cheap (band A) and include a guided tour of the Mill. The Bobbin Mill belongs to English Heritage and so members get in free, so remember your card.

STEAMERS

During the mid 19th century, if you were a rich industrialist with a house in the Lake District, the greatest status symbol you could have was your own yacht or steamer on Windermere. At that time the only ferry service along the length of the Lake was provided by two barges propelled by oar and sail. So it wasn't long before somebody had the idea of using a steamship as a ferry to attract the tourists now arriving in great numbers.

The first passenger steamship to appear on the Lake was *The Lady of the Lake* in 1846. A cruise on this paddle steamer cost the princely sum of one shilling on deck and an extra 6d if you wanted to go into the saloon. The launch was not without its opposition though and many locals protested against the steam ferry on the grounds that it would ruin their potted char trade. However, protests were ignored and a year later another paddle steamer, *The Lord of the Isles,* was launched spurred on by the arrival of more tourists at the newly opened train station in Windermere. Three years later the first iron ships, *The Firefly* and *The Dragonfly,* built at Low Wood, were launched by a rival company. There was bitter rivalry between the two with price wars cutting the cost to 3d for a round trip. The rivalry did not last long for in 1858 the companies merged and this new firm launched the first screw steamer, *The Swan,* in 1869. This was followed by *The Tern* in 1891 and *The Swift* in 1900.

Other boats came and went, but the original *Tern* is still in use with *The Swan* and *The Teal* being replaced in the 1930s with boats of the same name. All three boats still plough up and down the lake from Watershead at Ambleside, to Bowness, to Lakeside and back again. All three belong to the Iron Steamboat Company and though there are several other boat companies vying for trade on the lake, the large, white steamboats are still the most popular.

From Lakeside you can take a steamer every hour travelling to Bowness in 40 minutes and to Ambleside in $1^1/_2$ hours. A cruise up the lake of Windermere, England's longest stretch of water, is definitely a relaxing way to travel and view the scenery. It could also be combined with a visit to Ambleside or Bowness (though remember you will be walking to Bowness later) for a full day out. Alternatively you could combine it with a ride on the Lakeside to Haverthwaite steam railway.

Sailing Times: During high season (May to September) there is a sailing nearly every hour. In early and late season (April to May and September to November) this is reduced to every two hours. For more information Tel. Newby Bridge (05395) 31188.

Fares: Prices vary depending on your destination, although the cost of a round trip to either Bowness or Ambleside falls into band B.

STEAM RAILWAY

Following the success of the train station at Windermere and the popularity of the Lake Steamers, the Furness Railway Company decided to build a branch line from Plumpton Junction near Ulverston to Lakeside. The line was opened in 1869 with a new rail and boat terminus consisting of three long platforms and an ornamental station, built at Lakeside. Daytrippers could now arrive by train in the morning, have lunch in Bowness and tea in Ambleside before returning home on the train from Windermere. This became so successful that in 1872 the Furness Railway Company took over the Steamer Company and introduced four new vessels.

The line survived until the Beeching cuts, although a band of local enthusiasts formed the Steam Railway Company and reopened the line from Lakeside to Haverthwaite a few years later. You can now travel as those early tourists did on the grand splendour of the steam train to arrive in time to board the north bound steamers up the lake. Alternatively, you could travel in the opposite direction along the River Leven to Haverthwaite and visit the collection of trains and the station restaurant. Though this is not a journey to be taken by people in a hurry. The journey time for the full $3^1/_2$ mile trip from Haverthwaite to Lakeside is 20 minutes, with the short trip between Newby Bridge station and Lakeside taking just over 5 minutes. This gives you plenty of time to admire the scenery as it glides slowly past your window.

Opening Times: Trains run from April to November on a timetable which coincides with the running of the steamers from Lakeside, though there is generally more than one an hour. There are just three stations on the line; Haverthwaite, Newby Bridge and Lakeside. For more information Tel. Newby Bridge (05395) 31594.

Fares: Fares are relatively cheap. A single ticket for the full $3^1/_2$ mile trip falling into band A and a return into band B. If travelling on the steamer, there are a combination of tickets you can get which work out cheaper still, including a special Lakeland Link which includes a trip by bus to Holker Hall.

BIGLAND HALL

Perhaps you've always wanted to be part of the country gentry and take part in traditional country sports. If so, then Bigland Hall can let you fulfil your wishes.

Bigland Hall

Bigland Hall stands in 1,000 acres of private land with its own 13 acre tarn. Dating, in part, from 1125 this large country house has established itself as a first class country sports estate offering riding, shooting, fishing and more to anybody who wishes to try their hand. The Hall has its own riding centre offering pony trekking for beginners or parkland and cross-country courses for the more experienced. There is even an indoor riding school providing lessons to suit individual abilities. If shooting is more your cup of tea, then Bigland provides. You can try your hand (or rather shoulder!) at clay pigeon shooting with down-the-line and sporting shooting. If you wish to try the real thing then there is game shooting during the season (November to January). Alternatively you could swop your shotgun for a bow and arrow and have a go at archery.

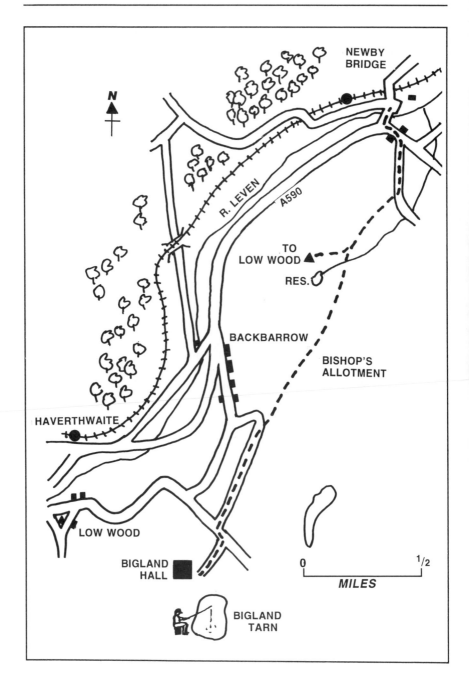

Fishing is supposedly the most popular sport in Britain and Bigland Hall offers both coarse and fly fishing. Coarse fishermen can enjoy all year round angling on the 13 acre tarn with day and evening permits on sale as well as equipment hire. There is even full instruction should you need it. If you prefer fly fishing then you could pit your skills against the trout at the nearby 16 acre trout lake. Again permits, equipment and tuition can all be obtained.

For those of you who wish to shoot deer – with a camera – deer watching expeditions are another activity provided by the Bigland Hall estate. Here you can get some close-up shots of the deer with expert advice. All in all, Bigland offers everything for the country sports enthusiast and all activities are closely supervised with full instruction when required. In this way Bigland keeps safety a priority. If you are interested you will need to book your activity before turning up at the Hall. For more information Tel. Newby Bridge (05395) 31728.

Getting There: Bigland Hall lies next to Bigland Tarn which we passed on the main walk. We could retrace our steps to the Hall, but there is a shorter route cutting the distance down to $2^1/_2$ miles.

From Newby Bridge retrace your steps from the main walk, up the road until you reach the track on your right which you came down yesterday. Turn right to follow the track uphill until you reach the stone stile in the wall. Go over the stile and continue straight ahead on the clear track (away from the track to the right which you arrived on) until you reach a ladder stile in the opposite wall. Go over this and continue on the clear track straight ahead for quarter of a mile and downhill until it leads to the road on the opposite side of this long allotment. Turn left on the road and follow it to the junction. Here turn left and then right into the entrance to Bigland Hall. Follow the drive for quarter of a mile up to the Hall and tarn.

Opening Times: Bigland Hall is open all year round, providing most activities throughout the year.

Prices: Prices vary according to the activity and time spent on them. The cheapest activity is coarse fishing where a full day's fishing with permit and rod hire will work out in band C. Trout fishing will cost slightly more with riding and shooting slightly more again. The most expensive activity is deer watching (band F).

MERE MOUNTAINS

Whereas Bigland Hall offers country activities of the traditional kind, Mere Mountains offers the more modern pursuits of rock climbing, abseiling, canoeing and many other ways of providing thrills and excitement which you will want to do again and again. Mere Mountains are based in Finsthwaite near Newby Bridge, but use local features such as White Scar and Windermere for their sessions and courses. They also travel much further afield when necessary, such as the Yorkshire Dales for the caving expeditions. Amongst the many things you can have a go at are rock climbing, abseiling, ghyll scrambling, canoeing, caving, mountain biking and much, much more. You could do a half day session of one of the mentioned activities, or a full day activity such as a day in the mountains, or a canoe expedition up Windermere or even a day of combined activities where you may be hanging from a rope one minute and pedalling your bike the next. The variety is endless. All activities are tailored to suit your own needs or the needs of the group and all are carried out under expert, but friendly, guidance from qualified instructors. Safety is of the highest standard and full insurance is carried.

Mere Mountains caters for all levels from beginners to the more experienced, so don't be afraid if you've never done anything like it before. It really does provide an exhilarating thrill and a fantastic sense of achievement to learn how to abseil, or canoe, or successfully climb a 100 foot rock face and it's something you won't do on many other long distance walks.

Getting There: As stated, the activities are based at various locations around the area. However, Mere Mountains will pick you up from the garage at Newby Bridge and take you on to the activity site. It is important to ring in advance to arrange the activity and time of pick up. The staff are helpful and friendly. For more information Tel. Newby Bridge (05395) 31000.

Opening Times: Mere Mountains offer activities throughout the year.

Prices: Prices vary according to activity and numbers. Obviously a one-off activity for one person is more expensive than for a group. In general prices range from bands D to F although this does include all equipment, instruction and transport when required.

LAKELAND 4X4 EXPERIENCE

Over the past few years 4-wheel drive vehicles have become popular, not just with farmers and landowners, but with more ordinary folk. This has been fed by the car industry with a whole range of monster sized, 'off the road' vehicles. The trouble is, the nearest most of these cars get to 'off the road' is when they park on the pavement.

Lakeland 4X4 Experience is designed to allow the owners of these new, shiny 4X4s the chance to get mud on their wheels. You can, however, hire a vehicle from the organisers and take off on their one day course – 'The Ultimate Experience In Off Road Driving Tuition' as they call it.

The 4X4 Experience is based at the Whitewater Hotel in Backbarrow and they have their own completely natural course set in 100 acres of fellside and woodland. The day's course includes a comprehensive training package allowing the driver to learn the capabilities of his or her vehicle in various terrains and conditions. This includes steering, clutch control, winching, fording and gear selection. The course also includes an educational programme called 'Tread Lightly' on the responsibilities of off road drivers to the countryside.

Getting There: The Experience is based at the Whitewater Hotel in Backbarrow and this is also the meeting point for the day's course members. You need to be there by 9.30 a.m., so although you could retrace your steps from yesterday and walk there, you would have to set out pretty early. No, better to get a taxi from Newby Bridge. After all the cost of a taxi will be little compared to the price of the course!

Opening Times: Lakeland 4X4 Experience offers courses all year round.

Prices: Very expensive. If you wish to take a full day course, with hire of a vehicle you are talking not in tens but in hundreds of pounds. For more information Tel. Newby Bridge (05395) 30030.

FELL FOOT COUNTRY PARK

Okay, I know what some of you are thinking. All this shooting, riding, abseiling, canoeing and driving around in Landrovers is all too much for you. All you want is a nice, relaxing day by Windermere. Then why not spend the day at Fell Foot Country Park on the opposite bank of the lake. Fell Foot is 18 acres of country park owned by the National Trust with woodland, picnic sites and space just to flake out and soak up the sun in. There is an adventure playground for children, a bathing area for the swimmers and the Boat House cafe for the hungry. You can even hire a boat and go for a short row on the lake. Fell Foot is the perfect place to relax and rest your feet. Even the transportation to it is relaxed and leisurely since the only way across is on a small steam launch, *The MV Cygnet*, run by the Iron Steamboat Company from Lakeside. For more information on the ferry Tel. Newby Bridge (05395) 31188.

Opening Times: The Park opens at 10.00 a.m. and closes at dusk all year. The cafe, information centre and boat hire are open from Easter to the end of October. For more information Tel. Newby Bridge (05395) 31273.

Prices: There is no admission charge to the Park.

WALK DAY 4:
NEWBY BRIDGE TO
ULVERSTON

Route: Newby Bridge - Town End - Ealinghearth - Roundsea Wood - Greenodd - Mansrigg - Hoad Hill - Ulverston.

Distance: $9^1/_2$ miles.

Maps: 1:50,000 O.S. Landranger No. 97 Kendal to Morecambe or 1:25,000 O.S. Pathfinder No. 626 Broughton in Furness and 1:25,000 O.S. Pathfinder No. 635 Barrow and Ulverston.

Getting There: Newby Bridge is easily accessible by car, being situated on the A590 at the bottom of Windermere. From Junction 36 of the M6 simply follow the signs for Barrow-in-Furness along the A590 . The only way to Newby Bridge on public transport is by bus. There are infrequent services from both Kendal and Windermere with both these towns having railway stations.

The Walk

The start of today's walk denotes the start of our excursion into Furness proper. Once on the far side of the Leven, we stay in Furness for the next three days until the crossing of Windermere back into old Westmorland. The walk starts with a short climb above Newby Bridge before descending down to the Rusland Valley. From here it follows Rusland Pool seaward until it joins with the Leven. A short excursion back into Cartmel brings us back across the estuary into Greenodd, providing us with a close up view of the sands of Morecambe Bay. From the village of Greenodd the walk leads over and around the low hills north of Ulverston before climbing to Ulverston's most prominent landmark, The Barrow Monument on Hoad Hill. This provides you with a bird's-eye-view of Ulverston strung out below. A small market town with a lively, bustling main street which you gradually become part of as you descend the hill into the town.

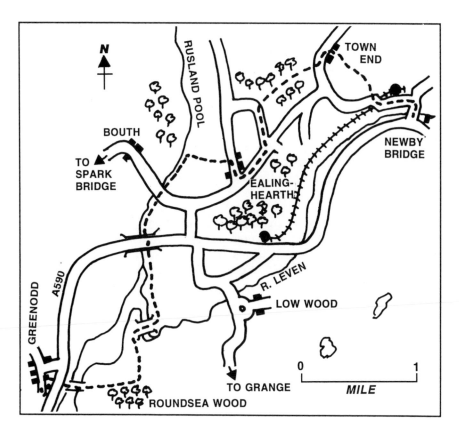

Section 1: Newby Bridge to Greenodd

From the Swan Hotel take the road by the river, signed for Finsthwaite. Follow the road past Newby Bridge train halt and on for a quarter of a mile to cross the bridge over the railway. Immediately after the bridge is a public footpath sign for Finsthwaite, on the right. Follow the sign into the woods and continue uphill on the bridleway. Follow this track for half a mile to a pair of wooden gates on your left.

Making your way uphill through this bank of ancient woodland, there is much to admire. Not only the imposing oaks and the spreading grandeur of the smooth lined beech, but there is also an abundance of smaller flowers with much to interest us. There is the small, creeping yellow pimpernel, a common plant of oak woodlands, and the blue flowered self-heal growing alongside the path. However, the largest and most obvious plant is the burdock. This tall wayside plant with its large, heart shaped leaves and thistle-like flowers is unmistakeable. In late summer and autumn, when the flowers have gone and the hairy burrs with their hooked spines are left, it is easy to see how the plant got its name - from the burrs and the dock-like leaves. The burr has been evolved by the plant to stick to the fur of passing horses and other animals in order to disperse the seeds through the area, but they hook equally well to jumpers, coats and even fingertips. In olden days they were used by young girls to throw at their lovers; if they stuck it meant true love.

Burdock has always been an important medicinal plant and it is still grown commercially for its roots. These are usually mixed with dandelion root to make the delicious and healthy dandelion and burdock drink which is an excellent blood purifier. Burdock has many other uses such as treating boils and acne, lowering blood sugar levels, curing falling hair and helping sore throats. All in all burdock is a very useful plant, but beware of young girls carrying burrs!

Go through the gates on your left and turn right to the stile over the barbed wire. Go over this then straight ahead by the wall on your right to the opposite side of the field and a track. Turn right to follow the track through a gate and downhill to Tom Crag Farm. Go through the farmyard and onto the road. Turn left and follow the road for 250 yards to a sharp left hand bend. Here there is a wooden gate by a public footpath sign and a sweet chestnut tree. Go through the gate and into the woods. Follow the path through the woods for half a mile, through three metal gates, until you reach a stile onto the lane.

The woods here are much more typical of this area than the woods before Tom Crag. A mixture of oak standards and hazel coppice these woods, like many of the woods on the Trail, would have once served the prolific iron industry of Furness. In fact, the Rusland Valley below us was once full of charcoal burners producing one of the raw materials for iron smelting. The different management of these woods gives us a different ground flora and amongst the plants to be seen are the small yellow tubes of the cow wheat, a semi-parasitic plant of woodlands. Other flowers include the foxglove and broom.

On the lane turn left for 150 yards to the junction. Here turn right following the sign for Haverthwaite and continue for quarter of a mile to the next road junction by a small group of houses. This is Ealinghearth which gets its name from the old hearths of the 18th century. These were used to burn the local coppiced wood for the fulling of cloth. Here you will also get today's first sighting of the Barrow Monument, the great lighthouse standing atop Hoad Hill. This will be your companion for the rest of today's walk, getting ever bigger as you near Ulverston.

At the junction turn right to follow the Rusland sign and after 150 yards, turn left to follow the public footpath sign for Bouth. Follow the path by the coppice woodland full of whinberries to a stile into a field. Go over the stile and continue to the end of the woodland edge. Here turn half left across an open field to the wooden gates by the river bridge.

This is the Rusland Valley, not the most scenic or most famous Lakeland valley, but it does possess a certain charm, squeezed as it is between the wooded fells of Furness. It even has its own historic house, Rusland Hall, to be found further up the valley. This Georgian manor house, set in 18th century gardens also holds the 'World of Mechanical Music' collection.

Do not cross the bridge but turn left along the embankment and follow the river for 1 mile to the road.

The river is Rusland Pool, though here it looks more like a large ditch than a river as it flows downstream trapped between large, man made embankments. These have been built to prevent the flooding of the surrounding farmland. Along the embankment there are few flowers, though horse-tail grows in profusion. This small, erect fern is the direct descendant of the tree sized ferns which once formed prehistoric 'forests'. In medieval times the horse-tail was known as pewterwort because of its reputation for polishing metal. Indeed, a few stems rubbed against any tarnished metal will soon restore its shine. The fern also has important medicinal properties and is used for strengthening veins, for guarding against fatty deposits building up in the arteries and for helping in cystitis and kidney stones.

Turn right on the road to the public footpath sign on the left. Turn left and follow the sign along the path by the river. Continue on the path to the A590. Carefully cross the busy A590 to the public footpath sign opposite. Follow this through the bushes to the path by the river again. Walk along the path for quarter of a mile to the footbridge and ladder stile on your left.

As you have follow Rusland Pool downstream towards the sea, the vegetation has been changing and here, on the south side of the trunk road, the grassland becomes almost swamp-like in its appearance. Around you are reeds, tall grasses and other wetland plants. The reeds which seem to make up most of the plants on your left is the common reed, *Phragmites*, but dotted amongst them are tall single stems of a plant with a tight cluster of purple flowers sitting proudly on the end. At first I was at a loss to identify these unusual flowers and when I tried using my flora they keyed out as the round-headed leek. However, as this only grows in Bristol and Jersey, I'm probably wrong. I cannot then tell you what this plant actually is, although it's a leek of some sort. Nobody is perfect.

Go over the ladder stile and turn right over the small ditch to follow the fence on your right hand side. On the other side of this fence lies the river embankment which is dotted with blue and purple orchids, like discarded confetti. Nowhere have I seen such an abundance of this rare family of flowers. At the end of the field is a track off to the left. Turn left to follow the track across the curve of the river until it becomes a path leading, once again, by the river. You are now following the River Leven upstream, so for a while the water seems to be flowing in the wrong direction. When you reach the stile, cross over it onto the old railway track. Turn right and cross the river on an old bridge.

The railway is the old branch line from Ulverston to Lakeside, part of which is still used by the steam trains between Haverthwaite and Lakeside. This lower stretch of line has long since been dismantled, though the bridge here has been preserved to keep open the right of way across the river. Across the river in the opposite sand-bank, you will probably spot the holes of the sandmartin where it has built the long tunnel to its burrow. This summer visitor is a common sight, darting across the waters, scooping up insects on the way.

After crossing the bridge turn immediatly left on the path between the river and the woods. Continue on the path for 400 yards as it leads deeper into the woods to a lane. On the lane turn right and follow it for half a mile, passing out of the woods to a metal gate at a sharp left bend.

These woods are the northern edge of Roundsea Nature Reserve, owned and maintained by the N.C.C. The woods hold many different trees, although the most common along this particular stretch is alder, a common tree of wet woodland and a good indicator of wet conditions. The woodland runs along either side of the lane for quarter of a mile before fading into salt marshes and grazing land. The edge of the woodland is decorated with honeysuckle, winding itself around and through the the branches of the trees. The sweet, heady odour of its flowers attract many insects, but it is in the early evening when the scent is at its strongest. This draws the long-tongued moths for whom it is a particular favourite. Only they can reach the nectar which lies at the bottom of the long tubed flowers. Another flower growing by the side of the lane is the pink petalled century, with its dot of yellow stamens at the centre of each flower. The plant gets its unusual name from the Greek Centaur, Chiron who was skilled in the use of herbs. This flower was once famous for its healing properties and was one of the 13 'herbs of magic' of ancient druids. It is said to clear the skin of blemishes and strengthen the bladder of old people, though modern herbalists use it more to promote digestion by stimulating bile secretion and as a help for aneroxia.

At the gate go straight ahead, through the gate, and along the track to the stile. Continue straight ahead after the stile to another stile onto the new concrete bridge. Cross the estuary on the bridge.

This single arch, concrete structure was built, at some considerable cost, to keep open the right of way which once existed here when the railway swept across the sands. The railway bridge has since been dismantled but the footbridge gives a close up view of the sands and some idea of the vastness of Morecambe Bay's flat expanse.

Turn left at the end of the bridge to cross the River Crake by the dual carriageway. Walk down to the river's edge and turn back and left to pass under the road. Follow the path on the other side around to the left. The path leads behind the buildings and works to end up on the road at the bottom of Greenodd village.

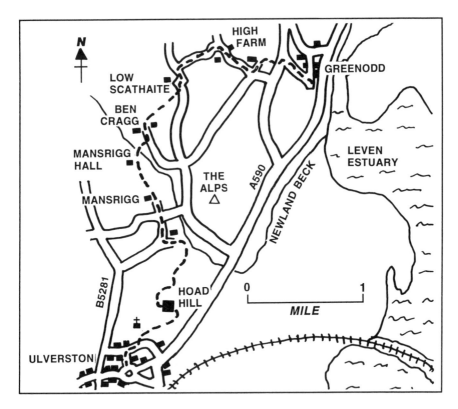

Section 2: Greenodd to Ulverston

Greenodd is a small and uninspiring village with not much more than a pub and a main street. It was once very different, for the village was once a busy shipbuilding port. When the Vikings first arrived in this area and moored their longships at the junction of the Leven and the Crake, they called the place Greenodd, meaning green headland. The village grew around the quay and in its heyday the docks had room for some fifty flats and sloops importing iron ore and other goods for distribution up-river by barge. Meanwhile, the port exported copper ore and slate from Coniston. The port even had a thriving shipbuilding industry turning out vessels of 300 - 400 tons. Its main claim to fame is the building of The Elephant, a square shaped box with an identical bow and stern which allowed it to travel in either direction. Unfortunately The Elephant turned out to be white and the idea never took off.

It is difficult to imagine Greenodd as a nautical town today, especially since the houses and main street have replaced the quay and the A590 cuts off the town from the estuary, but its history lives on in the form of the local pub - The Ship Inn. It is hard to believe that this once stood on the quayside of a bustling harbour.

Cross the main street and walk up the road opposite. Follow this for quarter of a mile mile uphill to the junction at Penny Bridge. Turn left and continue for 350 yards to the metal signpost for Smithy Green. Turn right to follow the path along the edge of the woods to the back of the farm. Walk behind the farm to the gate into the yard. Turn left in the yard and follow the farm track to the junction of lanes. Turn right and follow the lane uphill for three quarters of a mile as it bends around High Farm then downhill to reach another junction of lanes.

Looking around, the fields and pastures which surround you are mostly populated with cows. Whereas the steep mountain sides of the Lake District are the domain of the sheep, here cattle rule the land. The lush grass and gentle slopes provide ideal dairy farming.

Cows have a strange affect on some people. I have taken people on walks who would not enter the same field as a cow, let alone go near it and the sight of a bull would send them half-way across the county. On the other hand I have known people who would go out of their way to be next to a cow. I tend to take the middle line. Although not afraid of the beasts, I am still a little wary of them. One time I was leading a group of holiday guests in the Kentmere Valley. Half-way across a field we noticed a group of cows standing across the path and in the middle of them the largest bullock in existence. At least that's what it looked like to us. Cries of "Is that a bull?" and "I'm not going across there." soon went up. As leader, however, I was not allowed to show fear and with a fixed smile, promised it would be quite safe. I was pushed to the front of the group. "Okay, you first", they said. So off I set. The cows soon dispersed but that bull was not going to shift. Taking a deep breath and muttering "nice bull, good bull", I ventured towards it. I got so close that I could feel its breath on me. I gulped, closed my eyes and carried on walking. When I looked again, I was past the bull and safely on the other side. The group followed in silent admiration. I didn't have the heart to tell them it had been neutered.

At the junction turn left to follow the lane as it bends right then left to Low Scathwaite Farm. Here turn right up the track in front of the houses to a black metal gate. Go through the gate and straight ahead to a gap in a wall. After the gap turn right to follow the wall on your right hand side, through a metal gate and on until you reach a stone stile. Go over this and turn left to another stone stile in the far wall. Go over this and turn half right and walk downhill to the diagonally opposite corner of the field and a gate into Ben Cragg farmyard. Go straight across the farmyard, into a field on the other side. Cross the field to a footbridge, after which turn left and up to the farm buildings. Pass around the right hand side of Mansriggs Hall Farm to a gate onto a track. At the junction of tracks in front of the farm, take the track straight ahead, through the gate and continue on through two more gates. The track then leads by a wall on your left, under power lines to the far corner of the field. Go over the wall here and then follow the wall on your right, behind the farm, to a metal gate onto the road. Follow the road straight ahead for half a mile to the track for Falls Farm on the left.

Turn left up the track to the farm and then follow the yellow arrows down the bridleway through the trees. Go over the step stile then turn right and uphill away from the track by the stile. (This stile was specially erected in memory of Alec Lupton by the Furness Ramblers, though the stile is now redundant since the fence has long since gone.) Follow the wall on your right uphill, through the gap in the wall and then by the hedge to a ladder stile. Go over the ladder stile and continue straight ahead to a gap-stile in the fence on your right.

By now the lighthouse seems only a cockstride away, almost within touching distance. However, we have to go slightly away from it before approaching it from around the back. It seems a peculiarly cruel trick to get this close to the finishing marker, only to be forced to sneak up on it.

After the stile turn left to follow the fence to a wooden gate on your left. Here turn right, away from the gate to follow a faint track which leads to a wooden gate and kissing gate in the wall. Go through the kissing gate and along the faint track straight ahead which leads down onto a clear track heading left to right. Here you will catch your first sight of Ulverston itself, below you. But first, the lighthouse. Turn left on the track and follow it up to the monument.

Sir John Barrow was born in 1764 in a small cottage at the bottom of this hill. A bright child interested in astronomy, he attended Town Bank Grammar School where he made quite a name for himself. He even assisted in the surveying of Conishead Priory for the selling agents while still a pupil of the school. From school he took up work as an accountant in a Liverpool foundry, where he met a Captain Potts. This was the start of his interest in the sea and after taking a trip to London, went on to the Acadamy at Greenwich. From there he travelled all over the world in various Government positions, each time returning to his native Ulverston to tell of wonderful places, far away. Eventually he was appointed Second Treasurer to the Admiralty, which he held for 40 years. He encouraged Arctic expeditions, founded the Royal Geographical Society and wrote several books including the definitive account of the Mutiny on the Bounty. When he died in 1848 the local people decided to build a memorial to him on this prominent hill in the form of a lighthouse, to reflect his connections with the sea and exploration.

Today the monument acts as a local landmark, recognizable from miles around and a popular destination for Sunday walks. The hill offers some of the best views around with Morecambe Bay once more displayed, though never losing its magnificence, and the rooftops of Ulverston lying directly below you. The one blemish on this otherwise pleasant scene is the necessary evil of the Glaxo works. However, this obviously does not distract from the romance of the place too much, since scratched in the concrete at the bottom of the tower is a message of love. "And when you call, I will hear you. For my love for you and everyman will not shatter." Who said Northerners were an unromantic lot?

Walk past the front of the lighthouse to the bench and path which zig-zags downhill. On the lane at the bottom of the hill, turn right and follow the lane to the junction of lanes at St. Mary's Hospice. Here go straight ahead on the lane between two walls which leads past the church onto Church Walk. Follow this into Ulverston town centre.

TOUR DAY 4:
ULVERSTON

Accommodation

Ulverston is the second largest town on the Trail, after Kendal, and beds are widely available. There is a whole range of accommodation from relatively cheap B & Bs to more expensive hotels. Enough to suit all tastes and all pockets. You should have no problem in finding a room at any time of year, though if you want to book in advance you can ring Ulverston Tourist Information Centre. Tel. (0229) 57120.

ULVERSTON

We could hardly do a tour of Furness without visiting the capital of Furness itself – Ulverston. This attractive market town holds a great many interesting features and a whole day could easily be passed away in the town itself. Its grey, cobbled streets, busy market and real northern grittiness give it a worn but comfortable flavour.

The people of Ulverston are on the whole, friendly and welcoming, much the same as West describes them in 1779 in his guide to the area. "Furness people" he says, "and those of Ulverston especially are civil, well behaved to strangers, hospitable and humane. At church and market their appearance is decent and sobriety is a general virtue." However, I feel I must warn you of the other side of Ulverstonians as described by George Fox the Quaker in 1652. "The people of Ulverston are liars, drunkards, whore mongers and thieves following filthy pleasures." I will let you decide who is right.

Ulverston itself has existed ever since a Saxon by the name of Ulph decided to set up home here. In 1280 the growing town was granted a charter by Edward I and a market has been held here ever since. Ulverston continued to grow, despite being raided by the Scots in the 14th century, mainly due to its proximity to the sea and its links with the iron industry. Most of the iron exported by the Furness monks would

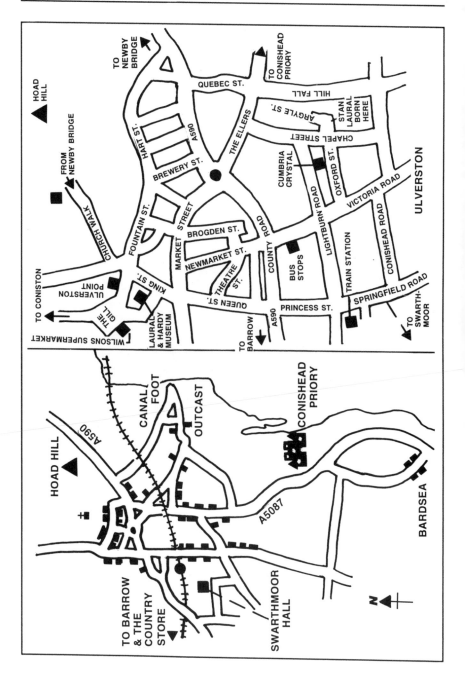

pass through Ulverston. The town even had its own blast furnace and foundry at one time. Ulverston's real boom period came during the 18th and 19th centuries and it remains very much a Georgian town, with its buildings reflecting this. This prosperity was furthered by the building of a mile long canal joining Ulverston to the sea in 1794. Built by John Rennie the famous engineer, the canal was soon carrying thousands of ships exporting slate and iron and the town's salty past can still be seen in some of the street names.

Market Day in Ulverston

The coming of the railway in 1846 made the canal redundant and the mile long stretch was allowed to silt up. The town gradually went into decline, with most industry moving to Barrow. However, Ulverston remains a thriving market town and the building of the Glaxo factory on the site of the old ironworks has maintained industrial employment for the people of the town.

There are many delights in Ulverston and a tour of the town, especially on market days, brings rich rewards for the sightseer. Market days are on Thursdays and Saturdays and it remains very much an agricultural market. This is especially so on Thursdays when the market is at its busiest and the auction market for the sale of livestock takes place. During Spring Bank Holiday, the Hiring Fair is still held in the Gill. This was once the time when farm hands were hired for the season but today is a modern fair of swings and stalls. In September the market charter is celebrated with a two week festival culminating in the Lantern Procession where local children parade their home-made lanterns through the dark streets of Ulverston.

The market square holds an impressive cross at its far end and although a war memorial, it acts as a very good market cross. Leading away from the square is Market Street, holding many extra stalls and at the corner of which lies the TSB bank with its ornate clock tower. Built in 1838 by George Webster, it has been described as the best building in town though several others rival it for the title.

Side by side with some of the more common high-street shops such as the ubiquitous Woolworths, Ulverston has some small stores and shops which are unique to the town and the run of alleys and side streets are worthy of exploration. Ulverston also has its own indoor market open every day expect Wednesdays. In fact the town has so many points of interest that several are worth a special mention here.

ST MARY'S CHURCH

A parish church has existed on the site of the present Church since 1111 AD. The first church, known as the 'four ones' because of its year of construction, was soon acquired by the local priory at Conishead. After the Dissolution, the Ulvertson parishioners used stones from the ruined priory to restore their own church. Today only the tower remains of their efforts, the rest of the church being rebuilt in 1866. However, even this did not escape unscathed having already lost its steeple in a storm.

The Church holds an almost unique feature in the form of its north west window, made of glass dating from 1805. Only in Salisbury Cathedral will you find a similar window.

CUMBRIA CRYSTAL

On Lightburn Road, to the south of the main A590. lies the old cattle market. The cows and the cattlemen have moved on and the sight is now home to Cumbria Crystal, a small factory of glassmakers. Here traditional craftsmen use full-lead crystal to produce fine items of glassware based on 200 year old designs.

Glass-blowing and glass-cutting, little changed from techniques used 300 years ago, are still the mainstay of the glassmakers trade. By visiting Cumbria Crystal you can see these traditional skills in action. You will see how experienced glass-blowers turn a molten piece of red hot glass into intricate and fascinating shapes using moulds and the power of their cheeks. The glass is then engraved by the glass-cutter and you may also watch this process taking place on your tour of the factory. To help you understand what is happening a photographic display explains the whole process from beginning to end. After watching the glassware being made you can buy your own piece of lead crystal in the Crystal Shop, selling many seconds at reduced prices.

Opening Times: The factory is open every weekday of the year, except Christmas Day, Boxing Day and New Year. It opens at 9.00 a.m. and closes at 4.00 p.m. on Mondays to Thursdays and at 3.00 p.m. on Fridays. The shop is also open during these times and is also open at Weekends.

Tel. Ulverston (0229) 54400 for more details.

Prices: There is a very small charge for visiting the factory (band A).

CRAFT GALLERIES

If crafts and craftsmen interest you then Ulverston is a small paradise. Not only do you have the opportunity to see traditional glass-blowers at Cumbria Crystal, but there are several galleries and craft shops in the town. One of these is Ulverston Point. This is a family concern based in Ulverston's old corn mill on Mill Street. The mill wheel and machinery of the mill has been carefully restored with the rest of the building and a converted granary being used to house a selection of water-colours, antiques, pine furniture, objets d'art, clocks and a strange collection of nautical items. This nautical theme is carried through the whole upper gallery where The Captain's Galley is to be found. Here you can enjoy something to eat or drink, though if you start to feel seasick the garden is available for refreshments. Tel. (0229) 56162.

Furness Galleries provides the craft lover with another gem of a gallery. Furness Galleries are based, not in on old mill, but in an old sherry warehouse and bank on Theatre Street. Many of the building's original features still exist, such as the recesses where the bank's safes once stood. The Galleries have a good collection of water-colours and limited edition etchings and prints. Its speciality though is the Doll's House Workshop. This contains doll's house furniture and large wooden toys made by the Galleries' owners and sold all over the world. A selection of doll's houses are often on display. The Galleries also have a small coffee room. Tel. (0229) 57657.

Both Ulverston Point and Furness Galleries are open most days (not Wednesdays or Sundays) and admission is free. In addition to these galleries, Ulverston also boasts a couple of antique shops which may also interest lovers of art and craft.

LAUREL AND HARDY MUSEUM

On the 16th June 1890, Arthur Stanley Jefferson was born in a small house on Argyle Street in Ulverston. Working in music halls and circuses, Arthur toured the country with his father. In 1910 he went to America where, sixteen years later, he teamed up with the vaudeville star, Oliver Hardy. The then Stan Laurel never looked back and the Laurel and Hardy films have survived as all time comedy classics. As a tribute to one of Ulverston's most famous sons, Bill Cubin, ex-mayor of Ulverston and committed Son of the Desert, has established the only Laurel and Hardy museum in the world. This personal shrine to the world famous comedian includes various films, tapes, Hollywood props from their films and personal items of the man himself. It also includes many newspaper clips charting the rise of Stan Laurel on his road to immortality. Considered a must for all fans of the duo, it can prove disappointing for some who expect more personal items but as the only tribute to Stan Laurel it remains a place of interest for all who wish to know more about this great man.

Opening Times: The museum is open every day from 10.00 a.m. to 4.30 p.m. Tel. (0229) 861614 for further details.

Admission: Entrance prices are cheap (band A) and are even cheaper if you can take advantage of the family ticket.

As well as the various attractions listed above, Ulverston holds many other places and facilities to explore or take advantage of. These include the Renaissance Arts Centre, home to the Tourist Information Centre and the Renaissance Theatre Trust who organise a wide range of shows and events (Tel. (0229) 52299); the local swimming pool (Tel. (0229) 54110) where you can relax with a little breast-stroking in a heated pool; or the Roxy Cinema (Tel. (0229) 52340) where you can take in the latest talking-picture from Hollywood.

All in all Ulverston has lots in its favour and little against it. This friendly, compact, little town offers a homely atmosphere with plenty to occupy the inquisitive or amuse the spectator.

However, if you have a craving to visit a historic house or you are getting withdrawal symptoms from missing ornate gardens, then fear not. Less than a couple of miles away lies the attractive, stimulating and historic Swarthmoor Hall and Conishead Priory.

SWARTHMOOR HALL

George Fox was born in Fenny Drayton in Leicestershire in 1624. His father was a devout Christian and churchwarden. George was also very spiritual, but believed less in the church and more in a belief that the true spirit was to be found in one's own heart. As a young man he travelled the country searching for like minded believers but all he found was mocking and even violence. Eventually he came to the North West where he began to gain many followers and the Quaker religion was born. The name was sarcastically given to them by a magistrate when told by George Fox that he should tremble at the word of God.

After travelling up through Lancashire, over Pendle Hill and along the Lune Valley, he arrived at Kendal. From there he travelled via Underbarrow, Lindale and Colton before arriving at Ulverston. Along the way he continued preaching to the locals, converting many to his belief, but many more were turned against him. In June 1652 he arrived at the home of Judge Fell, Swarthmoor Hall near Ulverston.

Swarthmoor Hall - the home of Quakerism

Swarthmoor Hall had been built here by George Fell in the late 16th century and then passed on to his son, Thomas in 1632. Thomas was a lawyer who soon became one of the most important men in the district. He was made Justice of the Peace for Lancaster and an M.P.. He was appointed many other high offices, including Judge of Assize for Chester and the North Circuit. Unlike most judges of his time he was extremely tolerant regarding matters of religion, though personally he favoured the Independents. He was happily married to Margaret Fell, herself a very religious woman and between them they had a family of 8 children. Unfortunately, Judge Fell's work involved a lot of travelling and when George Fox arrived on that June day, the Judge was away.

Margaret Fell and the children welcomed George, as they did all travelling preachers and Margaret was soon converted to this new religion by Fox's powerful beliefs and inspiring words. Many of the locals, however, were not as welcoming, especially the local minister, an Independent. When Fox went to speak at St. Mary's church he was thrown out into the churchyard and even Margaret Fell's protests couldn't prevent it. When Judge Fell finally arrived home across the sands, he was met by the Rector and a group of local men. On seeing them, Judge Fell feared some great disaster had befallen his wife and family. He was told by the group that his family had been bewitched by a wandering preacher, creating havoc in the district and that he must send this preacher packing or "all the County would be undone.". Judge Fell was not one to listen to scandal and sent the group away to return home alone and find out the truth for himself.

At home he found his family quietly subdued, but otherwise unharmed and he allowed George Fox to stay on. Fell himself never became a Quaker but he did allow Fox to preach to his family, hold meetings in the Hall and even to write his journal in the Judge's own study. He had great powers and issued warrants against any rowdies who abused Fox at Ulverston. With this protection, Swarthmoor Hall became the home of Quakerism – a centre for business and a safe retreat for Fox from his travels. From here Fox sent out his 'Valiant Sixty'; converted men and women who would preach the new religion throughout the world. Some of the sixty went as far as Russia, Turkey and America. Back home the Quakers were heavily persecuted for their beliefs. Not only were they thrown into dark, wet, disease ridden prisons but they were subjected to horrific torture such as the burning of holes in their tongues and mob violence. Many were killed, but still they continued to preach.

Fox himself spent many years in prison before he died in 1691 in London. Twenty-two years earlier he had married Margaret Fell of Swarthmoor Hall, by then eleven years a widow. She was now a widow for a second time and continued the spread of Quakerism until her own death in 1702. By that time the Society of Friends had become an established religion which was allowed to preach and worship relatively freely. Through time it has remained a small but significant religion with many important and benevolent industrialists having been Quakers.

Swarthmoor Hall today is considerably smaller than the one George Fox would have known. During the 18th and 19th centuries it suffered from neglect and parts of the Hall fell into ruin. Today it is back in the hands of the Friends and is visited by Quakers from across the world as the birth-place of their religion. All visitors are, however, welcome and even if your interest in religion or history are nil then this impressive Elizabethan house with its mullioned windows and panelled rooms is worthy of a visit for its sheer beauty. The magnificent four post newel staircase carved in solid oak is a piece of true craftsmanship as is the fireplace mantel in the parlour which carries the same passion display as the choir stalls in Cartmel Priory. In fact it is probable that George Fell and George Preston employed the same wood carvers, thus linking Swarthmoor with both Cartmel Priory and Holker Hall.

Swarthmoor Hall is a fascinating place to visit. A place where you can easily imagine those historic events unfolding. You can almost feel the expectant mixture of excitement and worry that Margaret Fell must have felt when her first husband came home to find George Fox in residence. A truly atmospheric house, it is near enough to the centre of Ulverston to be combined with a stroll around the town itself.

Getting There: Swarthmoor Hall lies to the south west of Ulverston centre, an easy and pleasant three quarter mile walk away. From the town follow the signs for the railway station on Princes Street (see map).

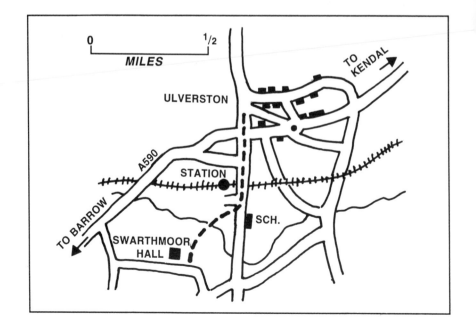

Walk past the railway station for 150 yards to a metal signpost on the right for Swarthmoor Hall. Turn right, through the metal kissing gate and follow the path to the next kissing gate by the 'Beware of Bull' sign. Follow the path across the stone bridge and then across the field to another kissing gate, watching for bulls as you go (these are much easier to spot than adders!). Pass through this gate and then follow the path by a superbly built limestone wall to a final kissing gate. 100 yards after this gate is a wooden gate on the left. This is the entrance to Swarthmoor Hall.

Opening Times: The Hall, as the board at the start of the walk explains, is open mid-March to mid-October on Mondays, Tuesdays, Wednesdays and Saturdays from 10.00 a.m. to 12.00 p.m. and 2.00 p.m. to 5.00 p.m.. You can visit the Hall on Thursdays or Sundays by appointment, but it is closed altogether on Fridays. Tel. (0229) 53204.

Admission: There is a small entrance fee (band A).

CONISHEAD PRIORY

Besides the well-known Furness Abbey, which owned and controlled most of the land in Furness, there were once two other priories in the area. One of these was Conishead Priory which dates back to the time of Henry II when it was established by Gamel de Pennington as a hospital for poor lepers. It later grew into a priory. It is said that the monks chose the site of the Priory, some $1^1/_2$ miles south of Ulverston, for its closeness to the start and finish of the over-sands route across Morecambe Bay. Indeed, just as Cartmel Priory maintained a guide over Kent Sands, so Conishead Priory maintained one over Leven Sands. Unlike Cartmel, Conishead did not survive the Dissolution so well since the locals already had a parish church in St. Mary's. The buildings were destroyed and used in part to rebuild St. Mary's Church at Ulverston. The site of the Priory passed to William Paget, then the Machells, the Doddins and finally the Braddylls. Many of these families built houses on the site though it was always known as Conishead Priory. In 1808 the then occupying Braddyll built 'a tolerable gentleman's house' at Conishead. In 1821 Colonel R.G. Braddyll began the building of the present house – some say for better, some for worse. The Colonel totally rebuilt the existing structure in a modern Gothic style, popular at the time, with the end result looking like an old set from a horror movie. It has to be admired for its sheer flamboyance. The outside contrasts strongly with the inside which contains some fine, decorative plaster ceilings, marble fire places and wood panelling, much of which is older than the building itself as it was taken from the Braddylls' other property, Salmesbury Hall near Preston. The Colonel's transformations did not stop at the buildings and he also had the surrounding estate of 200 acres landscaped. The woods on the seaward side of the house were 'arranged' so that from the windows on that side "vessels are seen in a most picturesque manner sailing through the trees". He even had mock, pseudo-classical ruins built on nearby Chapel Island just to improve the view.

Conishead Priory - the horror movie set

The whole project took 15 years and drove the Braddyll family into bankruptcy. The house began to fall into disrepair and at one time was used as a convalescent home for Durham miners. Then in 1977 the estate was bought by the Buddhist Manjushri Institute of Tibetan Studies who have returned the site to one of a religious use and are gradually restoring the buildings with help from grants and donations.

Though the Priory is a working college where people from around the country and indeed the world come to learn about Buddhism, the owners still welcome visitors and conduct tours of the house at weekends. In this way you may see for yourself Colonel Braddyll's vision as well as the work that now goes on there. The house stands in 70 acres of woods and gardens through which you are free to wander down to the shores of Morecambe Bay and gaze out towards Chapel Island and beyond. A visit to Conishead is interesting and enlightening though would not occupy a full day. It is, however, a pleasant walk by the shore to reach the Priory and could make a pleasant half day excursion. The Priory includes a shop and a coffee shop.

Getting There: It is possible to catch a bus to Conishead Priory by taking the bus for Bardsea and alighting at the stop right outside the Priory entrance. Tel. Barrow bus office on (0229) 821325 for more information.

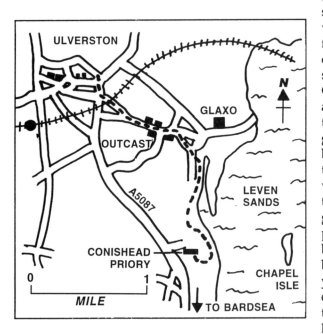

A much more pleasant approach is to walk the 2 miles from Ulverston centre, along the shore to the rear of Conishead Priory and approach through the grounds. It should be made clear at this point that this way into the Priory through the grounds is not a public right of way but has generously been allowed to you by permission of the trustees of the Priory. The house and lands are, in fact, private and no right of way exists on these grounds, other than along the shore. My grateful thanks go the director of the Priory for allowing this access.

From the town centre follow Quebec Street (see the map) for 300 yards before turning left down Morecambe Road. Follow this road for 1 mile as it leads through the small hamlet of Outcast and on towards the Glaxo works. 200 yards before the factory turn right down an unnamed lane which clearly leads to the Sea View Pub (a large, white building standing on its own). Outside the front of the pub, turn right down a narrow lane. Follow this for 150 yards to an iron kissing gate on your left. Turn left through the gate and then bear half right across the field towards the corner of a group of trees behind the house. On reaching the corner turn right to follow the clear path by the fence. Continue on the path as it becomes a raised track leading to a metal gate onto a lane. Walk straight ahead on the lane for 250 yards as it bends to the left before running onto the shore by a grey house. Just after the house turn right on a clear track. Follow the track which leads onto the shingle beach. Walk along the top of the beach until it leads into a clear path along the shore.

The Leven Estuary to your left was once part of the busy route across the sands. Having crossed from Arnside or Hest Bank to the Cartmel Peninsula, travellers would then risk the equally treacherous sands of the Leven to reach Furness. If the tide is out you will see the flat sands of Morecambe Bay, 120 square miles in all, reaching to the horizon. With such a large expanse of exposed sand it is little wonder that this area is so abundant in wading birds. Thousands of them are attracted each year and the Bay contains the largest population of over-wintering waders in the country. It is a relief then that a plan for a massive dam to be built across the Bay was never realised. In the 1960s an idea was put forward for an enormous dam to be built from Hest Bank in Lancashire to Bardsea just south of here. The plan was to create a large fresh water reservoir behind the dam to supply Manchester with extra water and to finally provide a road link across the Bay. Although the scheme had a lot of support locally it was thankfully never built. It is impossible to imagine this area without the sands and the environmental impact of such a dam hardly bears thinking about.

Follow the path for 100 yards to an iron kissing gate on the right, opposite to Chapel Island. Go through the gate to enter the woods of Conishead Priory. Follow the path through the woods and up to the Priory buildings.

Opening Times: The house is only open from Easter to September on Saturdays and Sundays between 2.00 p.m. and 5.00 p.m.. This is the time tours of the house are conducted. However, the director states that outside these times walkers are welcome into the entrance hall of the house where you can find displays and the shop. The house is closed to visitors altogether in the last week of July owing to the college's own activities. Tel. (0229) 54029 for more details.

Admission: Admission to the grounds and shop is free though there is a small charge for the house tours (band A).

THE COUNTRY STORE

Following the A590 from Ulverston, you soon come to the small town of Lindal-in-Furness. Here is found The Country Store, a factory and shop producing candles of all shapes, sizes and colours and selling them direct to the public. The Colony Gift Corporation has been making candles in this area for over 10 years and are the leading scented candle makers in Europe. They supply candles of all kinds to top-name stores such as Harrods and Selfridges. The candles are made using poured moulds or the more traditional dipping method, but either way all the candles are hand finished. At the Country Store you can see for yourself how the candles are made by visiting this beautiful and sensual store. I say sensual because it really does fill your senses. The first is that of smell. The heady aroma of wax and perfume hits you even before you reach the entrance. As you walk inside, the colours and sheer number of candles and giftware fill your vision and it is difficult to know where to look first. There are over 30 candle colours and as many candle scents. Twisted candles, straight candles, tapered candles, tealights, candlesticks, candlelamps, wicker baskets, soaps, ceramic gifts, glassware and much, much more are all here. One corner of the store is dedicated entirely to Christmas decorations and ornaments. This 'Christmas Shoppe', as it is quaintly called, is open all year round. The whole store is laid out in a 'country style' with lots of stripped wood and Welsh dressers and there are many bargains to be had. After your eyes and nose have been filled with different experiences, it is time for your tastebuds. In the adjoining Tallow Tubs restaurant you will find a menu of wholesome country foods to tempt you.

The store is an interesting and delightful place to visit, especially if you want to stock up for Christmas or that special occasion. It would not fill a whole day but is certainly worth a stop-off if you decide to visit Barrow on the bus; or maybe just as a small excursion on its own. I feel I have gone on at some length about the Country Store, but what else could I do when describing a candle factory other than wax lyrical!

Getting There: Short of walking the 2 miles along the A590, the only realistic way of getting there is on one of the several buses from Ulverston to Barrow-in-Furness.

Opening Times: The Country Store is open all year round, Mondays to Saturdays, from 9.00 a.m. to 5.00 p.m. and on Sundays from 1.00 p.m. to 5.00 p.m. (not open Christmas and New Year Bank Holidays).

Tel. (0229) 65099 for more information.

Admission: Admission to the store is free.

BARROW-IN-FURNESS

Barrow-in-Furness is by far the largest town on the Furness peninsula and it has built up around the port and shipbuilding industry. Barrow remains very much an industrial town, with not much intrinsic beauty but a lot of character. Sadly, the town is on the decline, not helped by Barrow's somewhat isolated position in the country. Indeed, the A590 has been called the longest cul-de-sac in the world. This is a shame, since Barrow and its people have much to offer.

If you are in need of a visit to a large town, then why not spend the day in Barrow. On the way into the town, on the left of the A590, is the famous Furness Abbey. Now much in ruin, this magnificent red sandstone building still holds a certain awe. Built in 1147 the Abbey and the monks who lived here, were at one time all-powerful in the peninsula. They established farms, built up the iron industry and exported wool to Europe. The ruins carry this power in the grandeur of the buildings. Soaring arches and enormous rooms can still be made out, although the monks themselves lived a simple and austere life. The Abbey now belongs to English Heritage and the admission price (band A) includes a tape tour of the site. Tel. (0229) 823420 for details.

Barrow itself contains many of the high street stores and shops you would find in any large town and in that respect is not unique. It does, however, have a modern sports centre with the latest facilities for those who want to take part in a sporting activity. (The Park Leisure Centre – Tel. Barrow (0229) 871146). There is also a nature reserve on Walney Island, across the bridge. Here eider ducks breed and the shore is home to thousands of seagulls. Be warned, however. Visit the gullery in the breeding season and the warden will supply you with a hard-hat to protect you from the dive bombing gulls! Fortunately the people of Barrow are friendlier than the gulls and if you are looking for brighter lights than Ulverston, then give Barrow a try.

Getting There: There are several buses linking Ulverston with Barrow and they are regular and frequent. There is also the train service, with stations in both town centres.

WALK DAY 5:
ULVERSTON TO CONISTON

Route: Ulverston – Broughton Beck – Gawthwaite – Beacon Tarn – Sunny Bank – Coniston.

Distance: $13^1/_2$ miles.

Maps: 1:50,000 O.S. Landranger No. 97 Kendal to Morecambe or 1:25,000 O.S. Pathfinder No. 635 Barrow and Ulverston 1:25,000 O.S. Pathfinder No. 626 Broughton-in-Furness 1:25,000 O.S. Outdoor Leisure English Lakes S.W.

Getting There: The only way to Ulverston by car is along the A590, whichever direction you approach from. For most people the approach is from the east and involves leaving the M6 at junction 36 and then following the A590 for Barrow-in-Furness. If coming from Coniston then follow the A5092 which meets up with the A590 at Greenodd.

Public transport to Ulverston is slightly easier than most of the other towns on the Trail, since it has its own train station. The line from Lancaster to Barrow skirts around the edge of Morecambe Bay and is the best and most relaxed way into Ulverston (other than on foot of course!). There are several buses to Ulverston, notably from Windermere and Kendal.

The Walk

When I came to plan today's walk I was already aware of the Cumbria Way which starts at Ulverston and leads to Coniston, before heading off towards Carlisle. The Cumbria Way was devised by John Trevelyn on behalf of the Lake District Ramblers Association. The idea of the Way was to develop a new long distance walk across Cumbria using existing rights of way. So, it came as little surprise that when I planned a route between Ulverston and Coniston using existing rights of way, it was almost identical to the first day of the Cumbria Way. You could say that great minds think alike, but try as I might I could not find a better way to Coniston without taking a massive diversion. In short, day 5 of the Furness Trail is also day 1 of the Cumbria Way.

Of all the walks on the Trail it connects the two furthest points, as the crow flies, and takes you from Low Furness to High Furness. It leads across bracken covered fells, past Beacon Tarn then down to the shores of Coniston Water. You are then lead along the wooded shores of the lake to Coniston itself.

Section 1: Ulverston to Broughton Beck

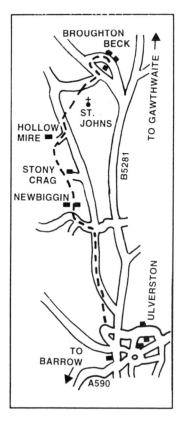

Start the walk from the Gill by Wilson's supermarket. In the top right hand corner of the car park is a signpost for Gilbank and the start of the Cumbria Way. Follow this sign up a tarmac path, keeping left at the fork. At the small stone bridge continue straight ahead (this is where the Furness Trail and the Cumbria Way part company for a while). Follow the stream until you reach a gate onto a lane. Turn left on the lane and follow it for quarter of a mile to the cross-roads. Turn left and uphill, taking the right fork at the wooden signpost, to Windy Ash Farm. Walk past the farmhouse then turn immediately right through the gate by the signpost (rejoining the Cumbria Way). Follow the wall on your right to an old farmyard.

The field here is an overgrown mix of dock, knapweed, bistort and ragwort. Though only a few ragwort plants are growing here, if not destroyed they could quickly take over this whole field. The problem with this bright yellow-flowered plant is that nothing can eat it since it contains poisonous alkaloids. This makes it useless to farmers but useful to herbalists. Gerard the Elizabethan herbalist recommends "the leaves stamped very small and boiled with hogs grease" as a cure for sciatica and modern herbalists still use ragwort for this problem. However, you should never eat ragwort or use it without expert advice. Besides, where would you find enough hogs grease?

Walk through the farmyard and along the lane following the clear Cumbria Way sign. Where the lane bends to the right follow another Cumbria Way sign straight ahead along a clear path. Follow the path through a gate, over a stile and then follow the yellow arrows to a metal gate by a power line pole. Go through the gate, across the stream and straight ahead towards the left hand side of Stony Crag Farm. After the gate here, turn left through another gate, then right to follow the yellow arrows around the farm, to another gate. Now follow the wall on your right to a small gate on the right. Pass through this, over the stone slab then turn left to follow the hedge to Hollowmire Farm.

St. John's Church

In this wet, almost marshy meadow it is no surprise to

find bistort, a dock plant which is common in the north west of England, though rarer elsewhere. Its tall clusters of pink flowers are a common sight in early summer and are unmistakable for anything else. When not in flower, the leaves take a little practise to spot but are worth the hunt, for they are beautifully edible. This is especially true in Easter when they are used to make the traditional Easter-ledge pudding. This consists of a small cake of bistort leaves and pearl barley, fried and served with bacon and eggs to produce a filling breakfast.

The name of bistort literally means twice-twisted and comes from the snake like root of the plant. It is the rootstock which is of the most value to herbalists and bistort has been used for centuries as a cure for bleeding piles. Today its gentle astringent qualities are used for many purposes.

Once in the farmyard turn right and follow the lane and Cumbria Way signs to a T-junction. Here turn left and along the lane for 400 yards to a wooden kissing gate and signpost on the right. Turn right and follow the clear path across the fields towards St. John's Church. In the last field, leave the path to walk to a kissing gate on your left. Go through this gate to walk between the house and the church to a lane. Turn right on the lane to the next T-junction. Here turn left following the sign for Broughton and then after 100 yards turn right along a lane into Broughton Beck.

Section 2: Broughton Beck to Beacon Tarn

Broughton Beck is a small collection of houses and farms, little more than a hamlet. As you come into this hamlet you reach a junction of lanes. Here head straight on past Saddleback Barns and follow the track to a pair of wooden gates by a beck. Do not cross the beck but turn left through a metal gate. Follow the beck for a few yards before bearing left to where the field narrows between two walls. Where the field is at its narrowest you will find a stone stile on the right. Cross this stile and then bear half left to a stone slab over the beck before turning left to a step stile in the hedge. After the stile follow the track which leads over a wall, through a gate then over another stone stile to a tarmac lane. Turn left on the lane past Knapperthaw Farm to a junction. Here turn right and follow the road to the next junction.

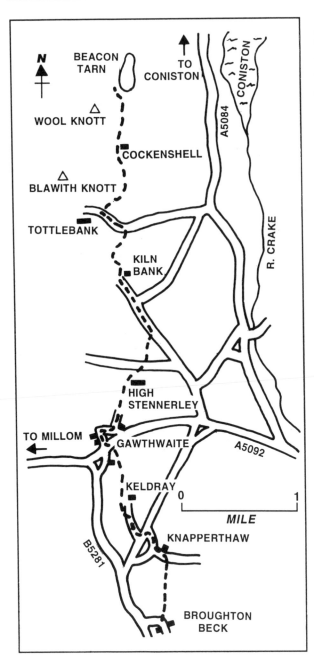

Along the road you will gain clear views of the mountains which lie ahead. Whilst today we look on mountains such as these as beautiful and inviting, when West wrote his *Guide to the Lakes* the mountains of the area were thought to be ugly, frightening and even threatening. Indeed, in his book West describes the hills of Coniston as "a most awful scene of mountains heaped on mountains in every variety of horrid shape". He considered the mountains and rocks to be totally unclimbable and it was not until the more adventurous Victorians arrived that climbing to the top of Coniston Old Man became a highlight of a Lakeland holiday. Today the Old Man is one of the most accessible hills in the Lakes mainly due to the old pack-horse paths which lead to and from the many mines and quarries dotted across the mountain.

Turn left at the junction then quickly right over the cattle grid. Follow the farm track with Bowfell and Crinkle Crags coming into view in the distance. At the footpath sign on the left turn to follow the sign over a ladder stile. Continue ahead to the next stile and afterwards right by the hedge to pass behind Keldray Farm to a stone stile. After the stile bear slightly left and uphill to a gap in the wall. Pass through the gap then follow the wall on your left to a track running between two walls. Turn left to follow the track uphill to the main road at Gawthwaite (A5092).

Like Broughton Beck, Gawthwaite is no more than a small collection of houses and farm buildings. However, it does have one small claim to fame. It lies directly on the boundary of the Lake District National Park and as you cross the road into the hamlet you also cross into the Park which we last left behind back in Greenodd.

Cross the road and turn right by the 'phone box on a minor road between the houses. At the fork turn left up the lane away from the main road. Follow this lane for quarter of a mile through three gates. After the third gate turn right to another gate. Pass through this then downhill to yet another gate before reaching High Stennerley Farm. Pass through a gate at the bottom of the hill and continue on the track as it bends around the farm and through a field to a tarmac lane. Turn right on the lane for 30 yards before turning left at the public footpath sign and the gate. Follow the path across the field bearing right, through another gate then keep right to a stile in the far right hand corner of the field. Cross the stile onto a lane. Turn left and follow this lane for 700 yards to a junction.

Growing alongside this winding stretch of road are many thistles, harebells and the small, white flowers of the yarrow. Yarrow is another herb historically renowned for its healing properties. In fact its name is thought to come from the Greek word *hiera* meaning a holy herb because of its many virtues. Its species name, *Achillea*, comes from the Greek hero Achilles who used the herb to cure his wounded men. Yarrow has been used for many centuries to heal wounds and in France it is called herbe aux carpentiers, who bind the leaves over cuts made by a stray tool.

Tea made from yarrow is light, pleasant and refreshing with the added bonus of lowering blood pressure, slowing the heartbeat and helping to clear blood clots. Yarrow also has a traditional use as a matchmaker. It is said that if a maiden plucks the flowers and places them under her pillow chanting 'In a dream this night, I hope my true love will appear' she will indeed dream of her true love. So I advise the ladies to pick some yarrow along this roadside, tuck it under your pillow tonight and find out who your true love is. Who knows, it might even be your husband!

At the junction go straight ahead past the sign for Kiln Bank. Walk up to the farm then turn right at the Cumbria Way sign and through the gate. Follow the track past the farm and by the wall on your left for 300 yards to a fork in the path. Here follow arrows to the right and uphill. Continue on the clear path across the hill to a gate and ladder stile. Go over the stile and follow the track left to the tarmac lane. Turn left up the lane to follow it uphill towards Tottlebank Farm. About 20 yards before the farm turn right on a clear track leading uphill through the bracken. Follow this to the crest of the hill then bear left to follow the track along the opposite side of the hill and eventually down to a wooden gate in a wall.

You cannot help but notice the bracken here. In fact, it seems to cover just about every hillside in view stretching away like a miniature forest. This quickly spreading fern is poisonous to grazing animals causing internal bleeding and cancers of the bladder. It is highly carcinogenic. This makes it a real problem for farmers, made worst by the fact that it is difficult to get rid of. It is hard to believe then that bracken was once highly valued and actually grown as a commercial crop. It was used for animal bedding, fuel and as a source of potash. As well as being poisonous to sheep it is also known to cause cancers in humans yet unbelievably it is still eaten in Japan and parts of North America where it is associated with throat and stomach cancers.

Go through the gate and by the wall on your left to pass the side of Cockenshell to a gate. After the gate follow the path down to another gate and stile. After the stile continue straight ahead on a clear path uphill through more bracken. Keep left on the path as it leads over the crest of the hill to Beacon Tarn.

Beacon Tarn

Section 3: Beacon Tarn to Coniston

As you come over the hill the vegetation changes from being mainly bracken to predominantly heather and in late summer the purple covered rocks suddenly part to reveal a small stretch of blue water. Beacon Tarn is a small, rather plain tarn cupped between the surrounding crags like a pool of water held in giant hands. On a good day it can look blue and tranquil. On a cold and rainy day it can seem like the end of the earth. Unfortunately the latter is all too common.

Follow the path around the left hand side (the western edge) of the tarn to pass through the depression at the far end. The cairned path then leads downhill, alongside a flat, marshy area before heading through a gap in the rocks and downhill again.

This flat, marshy area was clearly once a small tarn before becoming overgrown with vegetation. As the plants in the tarn died and rotted, the

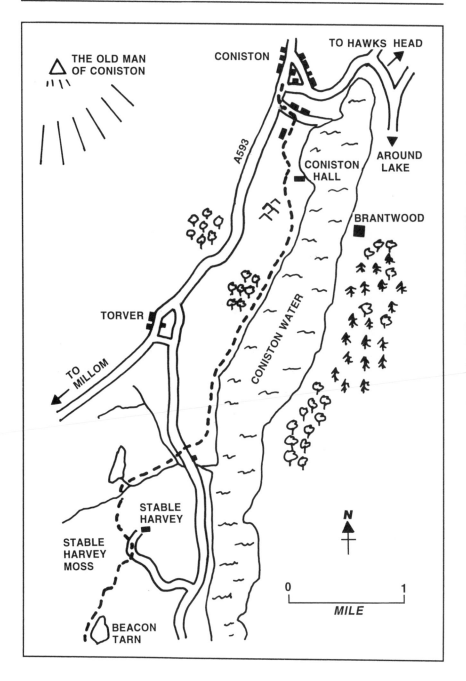

THE OLD MAN
OF CONISTON

CONISTON

TO HAWKS HEAD

A593

CONISTON
HALL

AROUND
LAKE

BRANTWOOD

TORVER

CONISTON WATER

TO
MILLOM

STABLE
HARVEY

STABLE
HARVEY
MOSS

N

0   1

MILE

BEACON
TARN

decaying matter would have built up underwater forming a wet, peaty soil. On top of this, more plants would grow, die and rot until the tarn became more land than water ending up as it is today – a swampy bog of rushes, sedges and mosses. At the far end of the bog is a small pool of water – all that is left of the original tarn – and growing from it the white flowered bog bean. This shallow water plant, would have been one of the plants which led to the death of the original tarn. Surprisingly, this is a good medicinal plant and is used as a tonic, a mild sedative and as a substitute for tobacco.

As you come downhill to a much wider area, the path becomes less distinct and you should then head for the tarmac lane on your right. Once on the lane turn left and follow it to the first public footpath sign on the left. Turn left to follow the sign along a bridleway. Where the bridleway splits, keep left around the small hill and under the power lines. After half a mile you cross a small beck. After the beck turn right to cross another beck and follow the clear track downhill with the beck on your right. At the bottom of the hill cross the footbridge and follow the path to the road. Cross the road to a track opposite, marked with a public footpath sign. Follow the track down to the side of Coniston Water.

In the 12th century this particular stretch of water was known as Thurston Mere, after the Norse god Thor. However, over time the name changed to become the same as the village which lies on its northern shore, Coniston. At $5^1/_2$ miles Coniston is not the longest lake in the District, but it is one of the straightest and calmest. It was for these reasons that it was chosen by Malcolm Campbell to set new water speed records. In the first Bluebird, Malcolm Campbell set a new record of 141.7 m.p.h.. After the war his son, Donald, followed in his father's footsteps by breaking the record five times between 1956 and 1959. On the 4th January 1967, attempting to break his own record of 276 m.p.h., Donald Campbell was sadly killed when his Bluebird flipped over. His body was never recovered from the lake and a memorial stands to this brave man in the centre of Coniston village. You won't find anybody breaking records on the lake today, since the speed limit on the water is just 10 m.p.h.. The Water though is still one of the most popular with sailors of all kinds and it is usually awash with small boats, dinghies and canoes and ploughing steadily between them all, the majestic steam Gondola.

Keeping by the lakeside, follow the clear path for nearly 2 miles as it leads through woods and fields until you reach a landing stage at the sailing centre.

The Lake District contains many lakeside paths, though not many better than this one. Here the old oak woodlands which once covered the whole of the area still reach down to the lake shore and remind us of the important part that wood once played in the history of Furness. As we have already seen many times, Furness was once an important producer of charcoal to feed the iron industry. The area around Coniston was perhaps the centre of early iron production. From when iron was first smelted in the Iron Age, the production of this metal was carried out in primitive bloomeries. This involved piling high a mixture of charcoal and ore, setting fire to it and then covering it with turf. The molten metal would drip to the bottom of the heap, leaving large lumps of iron behind once the fire had gone out. This method was simple but inefficient, using large quantities of charcoal to yield small amounts of iron. Such large quantities were used that it was easier to bring the iron ore to the charcoal than vice-versa. The ore would be brought by ship to the port of Greenodd then up the River Crake to the shores of Coniston Water and the heart of charcoal country. It is not surprising then that a great many bloomeries once existed along these shores. Evidence of these, and even early furnaces, can still be seen. In the 17th and 18th centuries, the building of brick blast furnaces saw the decline of traditional bloomeries and iron production moved to other sites such as Backbarrow. Now Coniston Water stands quiet and peaceful. Where once a constant smoke haze covered the water, now only an occasional mist descends to spoil the view.

At the landing stage, continue by the lakeside to a footbridge and a narrow gap in the wall. Go through the gap and continue on the track by the lake, which after a gate leads through a campsite and away from the shore before rejoining the lake after half a mile at Coniston Hall.

Coniston Hall is unmistakable as a large mansion house standing on the lakeside, most of all because of its large, round, Lakeland chimneys. It is said by some that these large round chimneys, found on many houses in the Lakes, act as a sort of status symbol. The bigger your chimneys, the more important you were. If this is true then the original owners of Coniston Hall most have been very important people indeed. And so they were. Coniston Hall was originally built in 1250 by the le Fleming family, who were sent by the King to overlord the area of Furness and quell any trouble. Sir Richard le Fleming established men-at-arms on nearby farms and recruited the locals to ward off the marauding Scots. The le Fleming family lived in the Hall until 1408 when Sir Thomas le Fleming married Isobel de Lancaster of Rydal and moved to the larger Rydal Hall. In 1815 Coniston Hall was turned into a farmhouse and is now owned by the National Trust, who are gradually restoring it whilst using the grounds as a campsite.

When I last passed the Hall in August, the annual Coniston County Fair was taking place. The campsite and fields around the Hall were thronging with people, many of them carrying their prizes from the fair's stalls. Alongside the track two men were engaged in the dry stone walling competition, rebuilding a small piece of wall. Dry stone walling is one of those things which looks easy but takes a lot of skill and experience to do properly. A dry stone wall is usually made up of two outer walls which taper to meet at the top. The gap in the middle is filled with small stones or 'heartings' and on top of the wall are laid the sloping 'cams'. The art of wall building lies in choosing the right stone to fit the gap. Because of the skill and labour involved, wall building is expensive and wire fences are replacing many old and damaged walls. This will surely be a sad loss to the country's landscape.

From the Hall follow the tarmac lane through the gateway then take the track off to the right. Follow this through a kissing gate on the far side of the field. The track then leads away from the lake before bending sharply right to pass through a wooden gate and behind a school. At the end of the track is a stile onto a road. This is Lake Road. Turn left and follow the road into the centre of Coniston village.

TOUR DAY 5 – CONISTON

Accommodation

Coniston is one of the most popular villages in Lakeland, though it lies off the main tourist routes and is somewhat quieter than Windermere and Ambleside. It has a great many guest houses and several pubs and hotels offering bed and breakfast to suit all pockets. Most of these are right in the heart of the village and are used to walkers with heavy rucksacks and muddy boots. You should have no problem in finding

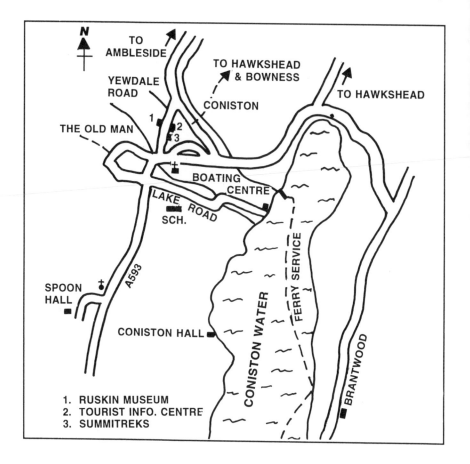

accommodation at anytime of the year. If you wish to book first, you can ring the Tourist Information Centre in Coniston. Tel. (05394) 41533.

CONISTON

Coniston village lies at the northern end of Coniston Water on an important geological boundary. To the south and east of the village lie the Silurian Slates where the countryside is made up of small, almost knobbly hills. To the north and west lie the Borrowdale Volcanics. These hard, igneous rocks produce the large, rugged mountains of the Lake District, including the 2,671 foot Old Man of Coniston, which truly dominates the village. It was the Old Man and the surrounding fells which supplied Coniston with its *raison d'etre* in the past. Once the highest peak in Lancashire, Coniston Old Man contains rich veins of copper and the mining of this precious ore, together with the iron smelting in the area, led to the growth of Coniston as an early industrial town. The architecture of the town reflects this history in its grey drabness, being more practical than ornamental. The village still holds a certain charm, however, and not many towns have a more picturesque setting.

Copper has been mined in this area since Roman times and the hills contain the oldest mine workings in the north of England. They were later developed by the le Flemings and in the 16th century began production on an even larger scale with help from the German miners of the Mines Royal at Keswick. Production stopped for a short while during the Civil War, then restarted after the Restoration. In 1758 the Macclesfield Copper Company took on the mines and production really took off. The town grew and Coniston saw its halcyon period during the 18th and 19th centuries.

At that time the copper was mined by shattering the rocks with fire and water. A fire was built to heat the rock, then water and vinegar was thrown onto the hot rock, shattering it. The rock was then prised away using hammer and pick. This technique was gradually replaced by the use of gunpowder, though the miners were understandably reluctant to use it. Once mined the ore was shipped out along the River Crake to the port at Greenodd to be exported to the rest of the country. In 1859 this was replaced by a railway line from Coniston to Foxfield Junction and the main Barrow line. This was the peak of Coniston's fortunes.

This prosperity did not last and owing to rich deposits in South America and the decline in demand for copper, the mines became uneconomic. The last mine was abandoned by the Coniston Mining Company in 1889. Today the mines lie empty and forlorn although the area between Coniston Old Man and Wetherlam is still known as Coppermines Valley.

By the time the last mine closed, slate quarrying had taken over as the main industry although this too was on the decline. The rail link to Coniston eventually became unnecessary and closed in 1957.

After the closure of the copper mines, the village went into steady decline until it found a new lease of life in the tourist trade. It has attracted many famous people, the most famous of whom is John Ruskin, the great Victorian writer and artist. The church of St. Andrew's in Coniston is pleasant though holds no special features apart from the grave of Ruskin who was buried there in preference to a tomb at Westminister Abbey. In terms of historical buildings and features of interest Coniston Village has little to offer the sightseer although its grey, slated buildings and homely pubs contain a welcome for all. There are several gift shops and cafes catering for the visitors as well as a good antiques market on summer Sundays. On the whole, however, Coniston remains a walkers' town – a town for the rucksack carrying rambler rather than the camera clicking American. For this reason Coniston remains a favourite with many. I think the character of the town is best summed up by the fact that the largest queue of people in the summer is not for any tourist attraction but for the town's fish and chip shop!

SUMMITREKS

As you might expect, Coniston offers more for the 'active' tourist than the viewer of stately homes and gardens. Many of these active pursuits are available through Summitrek. Summitrek Limited, like Mere Mountains, are a small company offering virtually every outdoor pursuit you can think of. The owners, Ron Rutland and Hilary Mills, have 34 years teaching experience between them in outdoor sports. They offer half day, full day and weekend courses in abseiling, canoeing, windsurfing, mountain biking, scrambling, map reading and virtually anything else you care to name. All the courses are expertly supervised and with safety a priority you can take on the thrill of an exhilarating sport in complete confidence.

Summitreks have a shop on Yewdale Road where you can pop along and find out more about the courses. It is possible to book yourself onto one of the courses here although it is best to ring and book any course in advance to avoid disappointment. All equipment and instruction are included in the price. If you are experienced in rock climbing or abseiling etc. and simply wish to go out on your own it is possible to hire the necessary equipment from the shop. The owners will provide expert advice and information on the best sites in the area. Summitreks also hire out mountain bikes for the day and half day, so if you want to take to the hills on two wheels then this is your chance. Sensibly, they also hire out cycle helmets to go with them.

Opening Times: Courses are run throughout the year. Contact Summitrek at 14 Yewdale Road, Coniston. Tel. (05394) 41055 for more information on courses.

Prices: Prices range from relatively cheap (band B) for the hire of bikes to more expensive depending on the course.

WATER SPORTS

Being next to a popular stretch of water, Coniston provides plenty of opportunity for you to take to the water in a variety of craft. You can hire canoes, windsurf boards, rowing boats, sailing dinghies and electric and motor powered boats for the less active. Whichever vessel you choose, cruising or sailing across the water is one of the best ways to see the area and is also a pleasant way to get around. The speed limit on the lake is set at 10 m.p.h. so even the motor cruisers chug slowly up and down. The water does get crowded in the summer but there is room for everyone and you won't have to dodge the large launches or speeding water skiers which can be such a problem on Windermere.

There are two centres offering craft for hire, both to be found at the end of Lake Road.

Coniston Watersports – This is a sailing and windsurfing centre offering canoes, dinghies and windsurf boards. You can hire these for the hour, half day or full day and all necessary clothing and equipment can be supplied. In addition full instruction and tuition on all these vessels can be arranged with the owners should you need it. Tel. (05394) 41760 for more information. Prices start at band B for the canoes all the way up to band F for the full day hire of a sailing dinghy. Tuition is extra.

Coniston Boating Centre – This centre provides no tuition but offers a wider range of craft for hire. The centre has Canadian canoes, rowing boats, sailing dinghies, motor cruisers and Mystic electric launches. All of these, with perhaps the exception of the sailing dinghies, are easy to handle and provide an easy and relaxed way of exploring the lake. Prices range from band A for an hourly hire of a rowing boat to band F for the hire of powered boats. The centre also has a cafe where you could sit and watch your partner rowing vigorously across the lake whilst you relax with a cup of tea. Tel. (05394) 41366 for more details.

Both centres are open from Easter to the end of October.

THE GONDOLA

With the increase in tourism in the Victorian age, Coniston attempted to attract some of these tourists away from its more popular neighbour Windermere. If Windermere could have a pleasure steamer then so could Coniston and the first steamer appeared on the Water in 1855. This was a small boat carrying passengers three times a day between Waterhead, Nibthwaite and Lake Bank. However, the idea did not take off and the service was soon withdrawn. It was not until 1859 that the idea was relaunched by the railway company who provided a service from the pier at Coniston which connected with the station at Greenodd. This allowed tourists easier access to the steamer and the lake. The steamer which supplied this service was launched from Coniston Hall in 1859 and named *The Gondola*. She was a small steam yacht described in the London press as "a perfect combination of the Venetian gondola and the English steam yacht". She was certainly very palatial in terms of decor and the Victorian tourists could now cruise the lake in style. In 1908 *The Gondola* was semi-retired and replaced by a larger vessel, *The Lady of the Lake*. Both steamers operated until the end of the 1930s when the service was discontinued. *The Lady of the Lake* was sold for scrap whilst *The Gondola* was broken up. Her boiler went to power a saw mill and her hull was used as a house boat. As such, she lay rotting amongst the reeds until winter storms washed her ashore in 1963. A little work was done to save her from the scrapyard but it wasn't until 1977 that the National Trust took on the momentous task of restoring her fully. After an appeal for funds she was taken, in sections, to the Vickers Shipbuilders in Barrow. Here she was lovingly and painstakingly returned to her former glory and by 1980 she was ready to relaunch. She was returned into service that summer and has remained a popular attraction ever since, combining Victorian opulence with silent splendour. There can be no better way of seeing the lake.

The service runs from Coniston pier, to Park-a-Moor at the southern end of the lake, to Brantwood then back to Coniston. The complete round trip takes just under an hour and you can get off and on at any of the stops. Without a doubt this is the best way to travel across the lake to Brantwood and the home of John Ruskin. It certainly gets you in a Victorian mood before you visit the house of one of the ages most prominent purveyors of taste.

Operating Times: *The Gondola* operates from the beginning of April to the end of October with 4 or 5 sailings a day depending on the season. The first sailing is at 11.00 a.m.. *The Gondola* cannot operate in rough weather and it is worth checking before hand with Coniston Tourist Information Centre if the weather is rough.

Prices: Fares vary with the length of trip but all prices are relatively cheap falling into band A or B.

BRANTWOOD

John Ruskin was born in 1819 and during his lifetime became one of the greatest influences of his age. He was an artist, poet, critic and much more. He championed Turner and the Pre-Raphaelites and compiled five volumes on Modern Painters which became the epitome of their day. He was also a great thinker and social revolutionary who challenged the moral foundations of the Victorian age. He wrote various essays addressing the working man, notably *Fors Clavigera*. His views on education were taken up across the world. He also took up conservation issues, something no-one gave much thought to in that industrial heyday, and as the original 'green' foresaw the greenhouse effect. His followers were many and included many great names such as Bernard Shaw, Mahatma Gandhi and Tolstoy. In fact Tolstoy says of him "Ruskin was one of the most remarkable men of, not only England and our time, but of all countries and all times.".

In 1869 Ruskin was elected Slade Professor of Art at Oxford and his lectures here, together with his social reform work, kept him very busy. In 1871 his mother, who had been a great influence in his life, died and Ruskin decided to move to Lakeland which he had known and loved as a boy. In 1872 he came to live at Brantwood.

Brantwood started life as a simple cottage belonging to Gerald Massey, who himself became something of a poet. From Massey it passed to W.V. Linton who extended it considerably. In 1871 he and his wife departed Brantwood, selling the damp, decaying buildings to Ruskin. Ruskin was said to have bought Brantwood, sight unseen, for the view alone. "It commanded" he said, "the finest view I know in Cumberland and Lancashire.". The view from Brantwood is, in fact, one of West's set views from his Guide to the Lakes. He even went so far as to recommend hiring a boat to admire the view better.

Ruskin lived in the house for 28 years until his death in 1900. During this time he spent thousands of pounds restoring and adding to the buildings and extending the estate until it included nearly 500 acres. The house was furnished to his own tastes and decorated with many of his own and his protege's paintings. Whilst there he suffered increasing periods of illness and was unable to work as industriously as he had in the past, though Brantwood is still considered an intellectual power-house and it was during these years that he produced his famous autobiography, *Praeterita*.

Locally, Ruskin was well liked since he was an extremely benevolant man, giving many thousands of pounds to various causes. He also introduced a new lace pattern derived from an old Greek design, which he encouraged his housekeeper to ornament the house linen with. Ruskin Lace, as it became known, was soon taken up by other local woman and survived as a cottage industry until the mid 1970s.

Today Brantwood stands as a lasting memorial to the writer and one I'm sure he would have approved of. The style and layout of the house remain as Ruskin left them with the study alone containing 4 bookshelves, a keyhole desk and an armchair all used by the great man. The house contains many other momentos including many of Ruskin's original sketches together with over 200 of his paintings. Other paintings include works by Turner, Northcote, Collingwood and Prout. In many of the rooms you will find period furniture especially chosen to fit in with the feel of the house. There is also a first class bookshop as well as a small museum dedicated to A. Wainwright. The Wainwright Gallery plots the history and work of another of the Lakes' great residents.

Nearby in the old coach house is the Coach House Gallery which is used to display and sell paintings and other works by contemporary Lakeland artists and craftsmen. Here you will find water-colours, oils, furniture, ceramics, jewellery, toys and much more which you can examine at your leisure. After all this you may feel like a sit down and some light refreashment. The Jumping Jenny tearoom can oblige. Named after Ruskin's own small boat, they serve anything from a cup of coffee to a full three course meal. The finest fresh food is used and the brasserie has a full licence. The Jumping Jenny has gained a reputation as one of the best tearooms in the Lakes, particularly for the tempting cakes and puddings and none better than the delicious sticky toffee pudding! If all this sounds a bit too heavy and damaging to your waistline, don't worry because you can walk it off afterwards with a stroll around the extensive woods and gardens which surround the house. You can visit Ruskin's Seat where the writer would sit for hours contemplating the waterfall, or follow the $3^1/_2$ mile nature trail to the peak of Crag Head above Coniston Water, or you could join an organised Garden Tour with a member of the Brantwood staff who will explain many of its unique features. Or, of course, you could always just sit and admire the view which is truly one of the finest in the Lakes.

There is plenty to see and do at Brantwood and combined with a cruise on the lake and a stroll around the gardens, you could easily spend most of the day here. During the season there is usually an exhibition or art course held in the house and you can find out more about these by ringing Brantwood. One day a week there is also a special demonstration of Ruskin Lace making. Tel. Brantwood on (05394) 41396 for details.

Getting There: Brantwood is situated on the eastern shore of Coniston, across the lake from the village. Without walking around the lake or swimming across, the only real way to Brantwood is by boat. This is by far the best appraoch anyway. As previously stated, you can take the majestic steam *Gondola* to Brantwood, though this does take you around the lake before arriving at the house and is restricted to a few sailings per day. Fear not though for the Coniston Ferry Service also operates a service directly between Coniston and Brantwood on a 1920s style covered launch named the *M.L Ruskin*. This has the advantage of half hour sailings and a direct service. The fares are slighty cheaper than *The Gondola* but it has to be said, it's not as stylish

Opening Times: From mid March to mid November Brantwood is open every day from 11.00 a.m. to 5.30 p.m.. The rest of the year, opening times are limited to Wednesdays and Sundays from 11.00 a.m. to 4.00 p.m.

Admission: Admission charges are cheap and considering the amount to see there, work out at good value (band A).

RUSKIN MUSEUM

For those who wish to know more about John Ruskin or do not have the time to visit Brantwood, there is a small museum in Coniston itself, dedicated to the man. The Ruskin Museum on Yewdale Road contains many of his original manuscripts and other memorabilia including the linen pall which covered him on his death. This was made especially by the women of the area and is decorated with the famous Ruskin Lace. The Museum also contains Ruskin's collection of rocks and minerals as well as general notes on the geology of the area. In addition there are old pictures of the local area and a feature on Donald Campbell's fatal attempt at the water speed record.

SPOON HALL TREKKING CENTRE

One of the best ways to see any area is on horseback. Trekking along bridleways and old pack-horse routes allows you to get away from the crowds and see the landscape from a slightly higher elevation. From the back of a horse you see much more than you would simply by walking and you don't have to exert as much energy. Spoon Hall Trekking Centre hires out horses to ride around the slopes of Coniston's fells, providing a means of transport ideally suited to the area and even more silent than the steam *Gondola*. The centre provides for both beginners and the more experienced, though all rides are accompanied for your own safety. Hats are also provided. If you have never ridden before you will find it both thrilling and enjoyable. At first the ground looks a long way down and you wonder where the brake is, but after a while you realise that the horse knows where it's going and what it's doing, better than you do. In the end you begin to relax, forget about the steering and concentrate on the view. Towering above walls and skimming the lower branches of the trees you can look down on your fellow walkers for a while with no thought of navigation or map reading. Trekking should be tried by everyone and Spoon Hall can supply horses of all sizes, so there is bound to be one to suit you.

Getting There: Spoon Hall is to be found a mile south of the village, just off the main A593. The easiest and best way to get there is by taking a short stroll along public footpaths to the Centre.

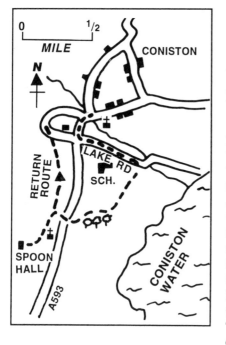

From the centre of Coniston, return down Lake Road to the stile behind the school. Go over the stile and follow the path behind the school which you arrived on the day before. Pass through the gate at the end of the field to where the track bends sharply to the left towards the lake. Here take an indistinct path slightly right to the clump of trees ahead. Follow the path through the trees to a stile in the far right hand corner of the copse. After passing over the stile, cross the stream to another stile. Cross this stile and follow the path to the road. Cross the road and turn right then left up to the Ship Inn. Behind the Inn is a car park and a bridleway sign. Follow the sign uphill to a kissing gate onto a wider track. This is the old railway line from Coniston to Foxfields. Turn left and follow the line past the white cottages and the church to two wooden gates on either side of the track. Go through the gate on your right and up the farm track to Spoon Hall.

For your return journey you could stay on the railway line which will lead you back into the heart of Coniston.

Opening Times: Spoon Hall is open every day from Easter to October.

Prices: You can hire horses for 1 or $1^1/_2$ hours with prices falling into band C and D. It is necessary to book in advance. Tel. (05394) 41391.

Although Coniston village and the immediate area provides much for the sightseer, only a short bus ride away is the picturesque and popular village of Hawkshead. We shall visit Hawkshead, with some time to look around, on the next day's walk. However, if you wish to spend longer investigating Hawkshead's many nooks and crannies and browsing round its shops, then there is a regular bus service between Coniston and Hawkshead in the summer. So I shall, for your pleasure, describe the delights and attractions of this popular little village now.

Hawkshead village on a quiet day

HAWKSHEAD

It is almost impossible to describe Hawkshead without using that word the American tourists are so fond of using, quaint. Hawkshead is the type of village every foriegn visitor thinks of when he thinks of England. Its quaint little, white washed houses line old squares and cobbled alleys which twist and turn until they disappear up their own entries. Its timber framed houses overhang the streets in a haphazard fashion, adding to the choatic tweeness of the village. And just to add to the feeling that the whole thing was, in fact, designed by Walt Disney, on a hill in the middle of the village stands the most English of churches, St. Michael's.

Having said all that, Hawkshead is a joy to visit, especially if you can arrive early before the coaches start emptying their hoards into the tiny village. You can wander freely through the village without fear of getting knocked over since cars are now diverted around the centre on a small by-pass. And there is much to explore amongst its winding streets and squares.

Hawkshead's name comes from the Norse 'Haukr's saeter' meaning Haukr's small farmhouse. Whereas Coniston's growth in history was industrial, Hawkshead's has been purely pastoral. In Norman times it was an important wool town made up of a collection of weaving rooms, small mills and farms. During the Middle Ages the Furness monks established a grange here. This gave them more control over this far flung outpost of their province. It acted as an important administrative centre from where they could deal with the copper, iron and wool trades which were a vital part of this region. Of these three trades, wool was the most important to Hawkshead. The Abbey was a major wool exporter to Europe and half of this wool came from the farms around Hawkshead; farms set up by the Abbey's monks. After the Dissolution of the monastaries the tennant farmers were allowed to buy their farms from the Crown and Hawkshead prospered as a market town. Its first market charter was granted in 1608. This was Hawkshead's golden period and many of the village's houses date from this time. By the end of the 18th century the shift had moved away from agriculture and towns started to become centres of manufacture. Here Hawkshead lost out. Isolated, with no easy access and no natural resources of interest to

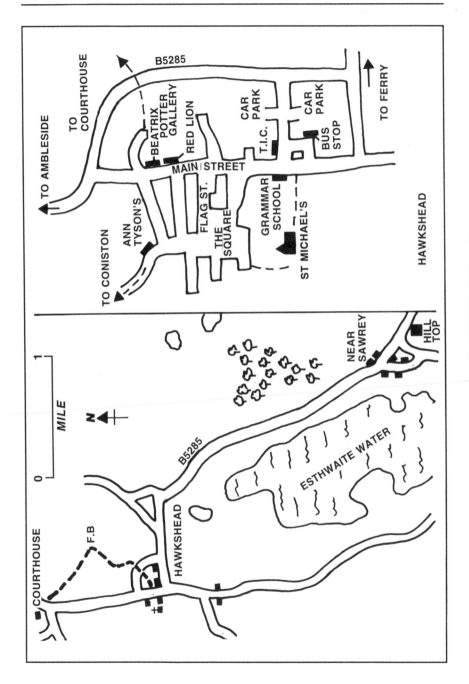

the new industrialists, the village stood still. And really it has stood still ever since and so remains a very small 18th century market town. Only recently has any building of any great scale taken place in Hawkshead. This building has been due to Hawkshead's new found prosperity in tourism. A large car park has been constructed at the back of the village together with a large slate structure housing a country clotheswear store. Other shops have also opened in the old buildings which surround the square, all catering to the tourists. A coffee shop selling tasty cakes and cappacinos, an excellent book-shop providing books of every kind, a kitchenware shop and gift shops galore including a National Trust shop. The Trust actually own many of the buildings in Hawkshead, a legacy from Beatrix Potter.

Getting There: It is possible to walk to Hawkshead from Coniston and we shall be doing just that tomorrow. However, this is a walk of 5 miles each way, which is probably best kept for the main walk. Instead, if you wish to visit Hawkshead on your day off, then use the local bus affectionately known as the Coniston Rambler. The number 505/506 bus travels between Coniston and Kendal via Hawkshead, Hill Top, Ambleside and Windermere. So it is possible to visit any of these popular places should you so wish. The distinctive green minibus runs every hour and is provided by Cumberland bus service. Tel. Kendal (0539) 733221 for more information.

Interesting as the village is, dotted around it are features and places which call for particular attention.

ST. MICHAEL'S CHURCH

There has been a parish church in Hawkshead since 1219. Before this the local people had to carry their dead to Dalton, 20 miles away, for burial. The present church dates from the 16th century, the rebuilding probably carried out by Edwin Sandy who also founded the Grammar School. It is a long, low building with a squat tower resting atop the hill above Hawkshead. Inside, the church retains some Norman-type features such as the nave pillars. There are several wall texts and murals dating from the 17th and 18th centuries as well as Elizabethan transcripts of the parish registers. These include over 200 'burial in wool' certificates an example of which hangs by the north door. In an attempt to stimulate the wool industry, an act of Parliament was passed stating that the dead must be buried in woollen shrouds resulting in many 'wool burials'.

Outside in the churchyard is a mock Anglo-Saxon cross which, like the market cross in Ulverston, is actually a war memorial designed by W.G. Collingwood earlier this century. The view from the churchyard is also quite a sight and there cannot be many better places to spend eternity. In the summer, music recitals are held in the church, most evenings. Ring Hawkshead Tourist Information Centre on (05394) 36525 for details.

HAWKSHEAD GRAMMAR SCHOOL

The Sandys were one of the local farming families who after the Dissolution in 1536 bought their property and became powerful and wealthy landowners in their own right. The most famous of the family, Edwin Sandy, was born at the family home of Esthwaite Hall. After being released from prison in 1554 for supporting Lady Jane Grey, he travelled abroad and was responsible for bringing the German miners to Keswick. He went onto even greater things and in 1575 became Archbishop of York. He never forgot his home village though and in 1585 founded a Grammar School here in Hawkshead. The present School dates from about a century later and has really just the one claim to fame – as the school of William Wordsworth.

William Wordsworth was sent from his home in Cockermouth to Hawkshead Grammar School in 1779 after his mother died. He left the school at sixteen, eight years later, to enter Cambridge before returning to the Lake District in 1799.

Whilst attending the school, Wordsworth, together with his three brothers lodged with Ann Tyson in Hawkshead. Today Ann Tyson's cottage is privately owned but a small plaque is attached to the outside of the small house to remind you of its place in history. After some time Ann Tyson was thought to have moved with the Wordsworth boys to Colthouse, half a mile away.

Both the Grammar School and Ann Tyson's cottage are visited as places of pilgrimage by fans of the poet. Together with Dove Cottage and Rydal Mount, they make up part of the Wordsworth Trail and can get crowded. Although Ann Tyson's cottage is not open to the public, the

Grammar School certainly is and this small building with its dark interior still holds that odour and atmosphere which old schools never lose. Upstairs is an exhibition on the history of the school and Wordsworth, whilst downstairs you will find their prize possession, a desk with W.W. carved into the lid by the young poet. This was something he was obviously keen on doing since he went on to carve his initials on various rocks in the Lakes.

The Grammar School is open from April to October and charges a small admission price (band A).

BEATRIX POTTER GALLERY

Wordsworth is not the only literary connection in Hawkshead and the name of Beatrix Potter is also indelibly linked with the area. Born in 1866 the daughter of a wealthy London family, she spent many happy childhood holidays in the Lakes. Her family would rent the mock Gothic Wray Castle on Windermere. She had a fertile imagination even as a child and would make up stories for a sick friend, Noel Moore, to amuse him whilst he lay in bed. Whilst away from Noel on holiday she continued the stories in letter form, illustrating them with small sketches, taking inspiration from her surroundings to tell the tale of her pet rabbit, Peter. Peter soon went on to make many friends including Flopsy, Mopsy and Cottontail.

Later on the stories and illustrations were laid down by Potter in the form of a book and sent round various publishers. All rejected her work but the author had faith in her work and in 1901 published Peter Rabbit at her own expense. Her self belief was justified and the book became a best seller and with the proceeds she bought herself Hill Top Farm at Sawrey.

In 1913 at the age of 47 she married a local solicitor, William Heelis and they lived together at Castle Farm Cottage, although she never sold Hill Top. She, like Ruskin, was a keen conservationist and believed whole-heartedly in the preservation of rural Lakeland. She knew Canon Rawnsley and was an avid supporter of the National Trust he had helped establish. She bought many estates and farms in the area, all of which she donated to the National Trust on the condition that they were always managed in the traditional ways. She was an expert on Herdwick sheep and made it a condition that all the farms could only stock Herdwicks. On her death she left the remainder of her land to the Trust, including Hill Top which she requested be preserved as she had left it and opened to the public.

The offices of her husband in Hawkshead have now been converted to a gallery and exhibition of Beatrix Potter's work – the work for which she was best remembered. Here original drawings and illustrations from the books can be seen together with photo's and displays depicting her life story. The original water-colours are beautiful to see and one can only admire the patience and detail which went into such pictures, now copied onto plates, mugs and other merchandise across the world.

The Gallery is to be found on the main street in Hawkshead next to the Red Lion pub. It is open from April to October every weekday from 10.30 a.m. to 4.30 p.m.. Admission is relatively cheap (band A).

HAWKSHEAD COURTHOUSE

In the days when the Furness monks used Hawkshead as their grange they established Hawkshead Hall as their administative and judicial centre. Here they would try and sentence Middle Age criminals. Today only the Courthouse remains of this 15th century manorial building and it is now used as a museum of local rural life. A comprehensive display of farming equipment together with an exhibition on sheep farming and how wool has been gathered and used over the ages gives an insight into the history and development of Hawkshead. Of course, any history of the area would not be complete without mention to coppicing and examples of bobbins, pit props and charcoal burning are also to be found in the museum. All in all the museum provides a fascinating look at the history of Hawkshead and Furness and accurately depicts rural life and traditions throughout the ages.

Getting There: Hawkshead Courthouse lies half a mile north of the village centre on the road to Ambleside. It is easy enough to walk along this road to the Courthouse but a much nicer way is across the fields to the west of Hawkshead.

From the centre of Hawkshead (having remembered to pick up the key from the National Trust Shop – see below) walk past the Red Lion and turn right by the public footpath sign for Latterbarrow. Follow the sign to the main road, cross the road and walk down the track opposite. Follow the track around the house to an iron kissing gate. Turn left after the gate and follow the track by the stream before turning right along the clear path across the fields. After crossing the second field you come to a small footbridge over a ditch. Do not cross this but turn left on a clear path heading back across the field. Follow this to the road (B5286). Turn right, then left into the Courthouse on the opposite side of the road.

Opening Times: The Courthouse is owned by the National Trust and is open from April to November every day from 10.00 a.m. to 5.00 p.m.. However, the building is sometimes used for local community events and you should check at the National Trust Shop in Hawkshead before setting out. You have to go to the Shop anyway since the Courthouse is unmanned and you have to get the key and let yourself in! Tel. Ambleside (05394) 35599 for more information.

HILL TOP

Two miles south of Hawkshead lies the small village of Near Sawrey. In the village is the famous home of Beatrix Potter, Hill Top. On one of her family holidays to the area her parents brought her to a rented house in the village which she described as "nearly perfect a little place as I have ever lived in". When her first book, Peter Rabbit, became such a success, she used the proceeds to buy the 17th century farmhouse of Hill Top in 1905. However, she did not live there permanently at first because even at nearly 40 she felt obliged to look after her elderly parents. Instead she renovated the farmhouse, built on an extra wing for a farm manager and visited it as much as she could. It was during her time at Hill Top that much of her best and most famous work was done including Jemima Puddleduck, Tom Kitten and Samual Whiskers. Many of these stories were set around Hill Top Farm and her fans will recognise the house and other buildings in Near Sawrey from her illustrations.

When she married, the house proved too small for both her and her husband and they moved to Castle Hill Farm. Beatrix Potter kept possession of Hill Top and used it as a private study and retreat. When she died she left Hill Top to the National Trust on condition that it should be kept just as she had left it. And so it remains, full of Beatrix's furniture, note books and other small belongings. It is almost as if she has just gone away for a while and the house is expecting her to return any day. It contains her collection of French dolls, her china and several of her paintings. It lasts as a memorial to this remarkable woman who gave so much pleasure to so many children.

Getting There: The Coniston Rambler, which runs from Coniston and takes you to Hawkshead, also runs to Sawrey and stops close by Hill Top Farm. This is by far the best way to get to Hill Top from either Hawkshead or Coniston.

Opening Times: Hill Top is open from Easter to October, Saturdays to Wednesdays. Due to the small size of the house, space and hence numbers of vistors, is restricted. Delays may occur at peak times. It is often better to check first. Tel. Hawkshead (09666) 334.

Admission: The entrance price is reasonable (band A).

WALK DAY 6:
CONISTON TO BOWNESS

Route: Coniston – Tarn Hows – Hawkshead Hill – Hawkshead – Claife Heights – The Ferry – Bowness.

Distance: $10^1/_2$ miles.

Maps: 1:50,000 O.S. Landranger No. 97 Kendal to Morecambe or 1:25,000 O.S. Outdoor Leisure English Lakes S.E.

Getting There: Coniston lies at the northern end of Coniston Water. The only main road through the village (A593) connects it with Ambleside to the north and Millom and Greenodd (via the A5084) to the south. It is also possible to arrive at Coniston via the ferry across Windermere and along the B5285 through Hawkshead. In fact this is probably the quickest route to use for most walkers coming by car from the M6. On leaving the motorway at junction 36, follow the A591 towards Windermere then follow the signs for the ferry. Cross the lake and on to Coniston.

By public transport the only possible way to Coniston is on the bus and there are regular daily services from Ambleside, Windermere and Bowness on the Coniston Rambler.

The Walk

Over the previous five days the Trail has passed over hills, through villages, across rivers and along paths and tracks. Although much of this has been within the boundaries of the National Park, you have kept to relatively undiscovered areas without meeting many other walkers or tourists. Today is completely different. Today you are cutting through, if not the heart of the Lake District, at least a major artery of it and you will no doubt encounter day-trippers, walkers and tourists of every kind. In one walk you will link up many of the area's most popular spots.

Starting at Coniston, a popular attraction in itself, we climb slowly through fields and woods to Tarn Hows, that small patch of water which appears on just about every postcard of the Lakes. From there we pass to Hawkshead village, awash with visitors in search of an idyllic England and a sheepskin rug, before crossing Windermere on the ever popular ferry to that very mecca of the day-tripper, Bowness.

Fear not, however, for this is a tour of the area and we should therefore be visiting the area's best sights and these places remain the best, despite the crowds. After all, why do you think so many people go there? Between the 'honey pots' you will quickly leave the masses behind and on the walk itself, will do well to meet more than half a dozen people. As for the walk, it takes in some of the best woodland around as well as some of the most expansive. It is quite a roller-coaster affair leading up and down from village to ferry, but it is a gentle roll that allows you to take things slowly and relaxed. There is much to see and many people to meet!

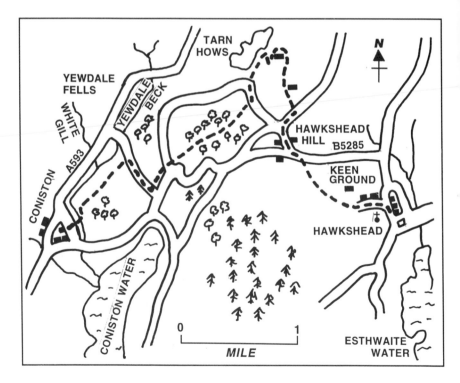

Section 1: Coniston to Hawkshead

Start the walk from the Ruskin memorial in Coniston village. Walk up the road away from the village centre towards Windermere. At the junction after 200 yards turn left following the sign for Ambleside. After a further 200 yards turn right at the public footpath sign. Cross the stone bridge and then turn left in front of the white gate. Follow the clear footpath across the fields to the 'ruined ramparts'. From here continue uphill to and through a gate then across two stiles and into the woods. Follow the path through the woods then into a field. Follow the path across the field and in doing so notice the cascading, white waters of White Gill Falls on your left. There are also clear views up the Yewdale Valley. Follow the yellow arrows to the gate then straight ahead to another gate on the far side of the field. Go through this gate onto a track and turn right. Follow the track for quarter of a mile, past the farm to the road.

Along this old farm track lies an equally old hedge and below it many hedge-side plants. Amongst them is the large self-heal. Large self-heal is at first sight a simple looking plant with oval leaves and violet-blue flowers, much like its smaller namesake. However, like many humans it has a complicated sex life. Most plants have hermaphroditic flowers with both male and female parts. This ensures fertilization, but unfortunately usually means self-fertilization. If the purpose of sex is to produce new genetic combinations, and the scientists tell us it is, then self-fertilization is not a good idea. Plants have evolved many ways of avoiding this. The easiest method is to have separate male and female plants. Some, however, keep their hermaphroditic flowers but have the male and female parts maturing at different times to avoid self-fertilization. Others have mostly female flowers with a few hermaphroditic flowers to be on the safe side and there are others still with every combination in-between. The large self-heal, on the other hand, just cannot make its mind up in which direction to jump. It has individuals with hermaphroditic flowers where the male parts mature before the female's and ones where the parts mature at the same time. It also has individuals with female and hermaphroditic flowers on the same plant and others with female and hermaphroditic flowers on separate plants. This is known as keeping your options open!

On the road turn left and follow the public footpath which runs by the side of the road. The path ends at a road junction. Cross the road and follow the path opposite, signed Tarn Hows. Follow the path through the woods, uphill for 1 mile. Ignore all paths off to the left and right and continue uphill until you reach the road above Tarn Hows. On the road turn left and walk downhill to the shores of the tarn.

A lone tourist at Tarn Hows

Greta Garbo in her quest to be alone would surely have never come to Tarn Hows. One of the most popular spots in the Lake District, you will always find company here, whatever the time of year. The reason for this is obvious. Tarn Hows is the prettiest, most scenic pool of water in the District. A large tarn with small islands and wooded peninsulas surrounded by imposing crags and fells with the peaks of larger mountains in the background. It is hardly surprising that a photograph of Tarn Hows appears in everyone's album. It is some surprise then that this beauty is actually man made, created by the damming of Tarn Gill to the west of the tarn. Before being flooded the area had 3 small tarns of little appeal. This larger tarn has now been landscaped with planted trees and 'artificial' islands where the waters do not reach and presents an altogether pleasanter view. I am sure the Victorian creators would have approved of the final outcome.

Because of the shallow water which joins the 3 deeper tarns, the new tarn freezes over easily in the cold weather and is a popular spot for skaters. In fact, Tarn Hows is probably at its best on a cold, crisp winter's day when the crowds are limited to a few skaters and the surrounding hills shoulder a scattering of white.

Follow the clear track around the east side of the tarn to a small sign for 'Main Path around the Lake'. Here turn right on the track uphill to reach an upper track above the tarn. Turn left on this track and follow it round to a small house (Rose Cottage). Pass on the left side of the house and along a clear path running parallel with the wall on your left. When you reach the stile in the corner, go over it then straight ahead across the track to follow the fence on your left to a wooden gate. Go through the gate and follow the path by the wall on your right. Continue on the path as it leads into a track between two walls. Follow this track downhill past the farm buildings and across the field to a road.

Passing through this field in summer you are bound to notice tall stalks bearing egg shaped clusters of purple flowers, widely scattered throughout the grass. This is great burnet, a tall perennial plant found in many wet pastures and once grown as a fodder crop. Medically it can be used for diarrhoea, dysentery and internal bleeding. Gastronomically it can be used in salads or in beers. Personally I like it just where it is since I think it is one of the nicest and most striking of grassland flowers.

Turn right on the road and follow it to the junction. Here turn left (signed Hawkshead) and follow the road to the main road (B5286) at Hawkshead Hill. Turn left on the main road, following the sign for Hawkshead and continue for 300 yards to a public footpath sign on the right. Go through the kissing gate here and then bear half left on a path across the field. Follow the path across a track and then straight ahead to a kissing gate.

When the monks of Furness owned this land they established various farms in the area and put in tenant farmers. These 'official' farms were termed 'parks' and can be recognised today by their name. Such farms as Water Park, Hill Park and Park-a-Moor were all once Abbey farms. Around these farms various squatters established themselves, clearing patches of forest or moor to farm the land. Instead of throwing them off their land, the monks made formal agreements with the squatters allowing them to farm up to $1^1/_2$ acres and build a homestead. These newer farms were called 'grounds' and Keen Ground, the farm past which you will soon be walking is one example.

This area was also the hunting ground of the notorious Castlehow Gang, a group of rough brothers who robbed travellers in the 18th century. They were big, hard men with great strength. One is said to have been able to crush a pewter jug like a leaf and any travellers of the day must have lived in fear for their safety. When the local bobby went to arrest one of the brothers he was attacked by the rest of the family with pitchforks and the brother escaped. His bid for freedom was short lived, however, and he was caught and hung in 1785. Despite all their faults the brothers were great stone wallers and much of their work can still be seen around Castlehow.

After passing through the gate, cross the stream and follow the path downhill by the stream and electric fence to another kissing gate. Continue on the path after the gate, heading downhill to the track from Keen Ground Farm. Turn right on the track and follow it to the next kissing gate onto a lane. Turn left on the lane and follow it downhill into Hawkshead village.

Section 2: Hawkshead to Bowness

You enter Hawkshead by Ann Tyson's cottage and the square. Hawkshead is a village well worth a look round and is described in more detail in the previous chapter. Even if you spent some time here yesterday you will probably find something else to admire and photograph, such is the charm of this village.

From the main street walk past the Beatrix Potter Gallery and Red Lion pub to turn right after the pub by the sign for Latterbarrow and Claife Heights. Follow the sign to the road and cross the road to the track opposite. Follow the track around the houses to an iron kissing gate. Go through the gate and turn left to follow the stream and then a clear path across the fields. At the end of the second field, cross the ditch on the footbridge and go through the kissing gate. Turn right for Colthouse. Go through another kissing gate and cross the track to a small gate in the hedge. Pass through this gate and follow the path ahead up the hill to a wall and stone stile at the top. Go over the stile then follow the yellow arrow to a stile in the opposite wall.

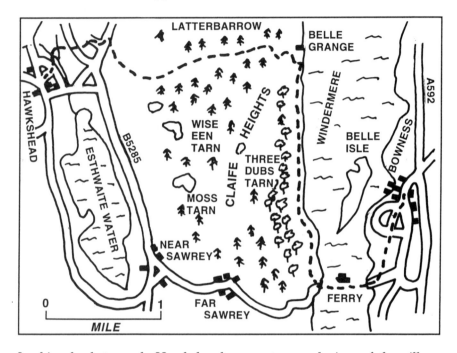

Looking back towards Hawkshead you get a good view of the village from here – a small cluster of houses overlooked by the church. To the left of the village is Esthwaite Water which means 'clearing by the water'. It is one of Lakeland's quietest and least known lakes. This is not due to its lack of beauty since in many ways it has a pastoral elegance which one would expect to find in an 18th century estate with quiet waters surrounded by grazing cows and a wooded background. However, its position between the mighty Windermere and the popular Coniston make it lost between giants and many people have never even heard of Esthwaite Water.

Go over the stile and bear half left to the opposite corner of the field and a gate. Pass through the gate onto a lane. Turn right up to the junction and then left. After 30 yards turn right on a track signed for Claife Heights. Follow the track behind the house and then on for 1 mile, ignoring smaller paths off to the left and right. During this mile you will pass through two gates, cross a small stream and towards the end will follow a muddy track between two walls. At the end of this track is a third gate at a junction of tracks in the middle of dense woodland.

This is Claife Heights, a small cluster of hills lying between Windermere and Esthwaite Water, mostly covered with dense woodland and dotted with small tarns. Most of the land here is owned by the Forestry Commission who use it to grow various fast-growing conifers as a source of timber. Because of this, although the paths through the area remain constant, the landscape around them changes dramatically. One day you could be walking through a mature spruce forest and the next through a desolate spread of tree stumps. Even when the landscape is constant the lack of landmarks as you walk between ranks of towering tree trunks makes navigation difficult. I know several very good walking guides who have got lost for several hours in Claife Heights. However, the paths have been clearly sign posted over the past few years and you should get out of here alive!

At the moment, however, you should be passing through the fields lying on the western side of the Heights, without too many trees to cause a problem. Instead you can concentrate on looking for the small, pink flowers of the lousewort. Easy to identify because of its hooded flowers and fern-like leaves, you will always find this plant in wet, acid conditions such as these. Like several grassland plants, the lousewort is semi-parasitic. Although it produces its own food with its green leaves, its roots have little suckers which attach themselves to the roots of nearby plants and pinch their water. The name lousewort, by the way, comes from the plants reputation for ridding the hair of lice.

At the junction of tracks go straight ahead following the sign for the ferry and Far Sawrey. Follow the track through the woods to another signpost after 200 yards. Again go straight ahead and downhill following the sign for Belle Grange. (I passed through a large deer gate here, erected to keep the deer out of this newly planted enclosure. However, knowing the Forestry Commission and Claife Heights it will have been taken down by the time you do this walk.) Follow the path downhill to a crossroads of paths (and another deer gate) at the bottom. Go straight ahead once more to follow the Belle Grange sign along a track through more trees. Continue on the track which after quarter of a mile becomes a cobbled bridleway.

You are now in the heart of Claife Heights' wooden maze and conifer trunks surround you on all sides. This is one area of the Lake District which I usually tend to avoid. Not because of the lack of scenery or the fear of getting lost but because I always get attacked by the dreaded clegg. The woods of Claife Heights, particularly on hot, humid days, are a happy hunting ground for this irritating horse-fly. About the size of a house-fly, this grey assassin is totally silent in its approach and the first you know about its presence is a small prick in your skin. Into your skin dive the two sharp daggers of its mouth parts, which are then pulled apart like a pair of shears and your blood comes gushing out. The clegg laps up the blood and once full, flies away leaving you with a huge, inflamed bite which itches like crazy. As you can tell, I dislike these cleggs immensely and never venture into Claife Heights without my insect repellent. If you have forgotten yours then don't worry. A good natural repellent is to rub your bare skin with elder leaves or a few drops of lavender oil on your hair will keep them at bay. Actually, I should point out, in the flies defence, that it is only the female which causes the problem, the males being totally harmless. No comment!

Follow the cobbled bridleway as it zig-zags downhill towards the lake shore. At the bottom of the hill turn right along a clear track with Windermere on your left. After $1^1/_2$ miles the track becomes a tarmac lane.

Following the track by the side of Windermere provides us with many things to see. Firstly there is the lake itself, gently lapping at the shore beside you, its peace only broken by the chug of a launch or the roar of a speed boat. Windermere today is very different from the lake that West knew back in the 18th century. At that time West wrote of the lake "not one bullrush or swampreed defiles the margin of this imperial lake". He even admired the buildings by the lake saying the modern dwellings being built along the shore were "works of art, most of which are in styles suitable to their situation". I do not think he would say the same of today's 'modern dwellings' which have appeared on the lake shore.

Along the other side of the track you may have spotted the change in woodland. The land here is owned by the National Trust who have more or less left the original broad-leaved woodland to grow to its full magnificence. As a result the trees that line this track are some of the largest and most impressive I have ever seen. In particular there are several mature sweet chestnuts whose massive, spiralling trunks form giant pillars of immense beauty.

Also on your right, in the hills amongst the trees, is an old quarry called the Crier of the Claife after an 18th century ghost which once haunted these woods. It all began, as do all the best ghost stories, on a dark and stormy night. At this time the ferry across the lake was a large row-boat which when not in use was tied up on the western shore so the ferrymen could relax in the Ferry House Tavern. If you wanted to use the ferry from the other side you would stand on the bank and shout across the lake for a boatman. This particular stormy night a cry was heard from across the water and a sober boatman answered the call. On his return he was alone, ghostly white and dumb with horror. The next day he was high with a fever and died a few days later without revealing what he had seen that fearful night. Every stormy night after that a mournful cry was heard across the lake but no-one would answer it. This continued until Christmas Day when a local monk was called to exorcise the ghost, now called the Crier of the Claife. He exorcised it into the old quarry and since then nobody will go near the site at night. Foxhounds are said to come to a full stop at the spot and not many years after the exorcism a local school master disappeared in this area!

Follow the tarmac lane for another third of a mile, through the gate, until you reach a public footpath sign on the left opposite a castle-like wall. Turn left to follow the path through the trees to re-join the road. Turn left and follow the road past the Freshwater Ecology building, once the Ferry House Tavern, to the ferry.

There has been a regular ferry across Windermere for at least 500 years. In the beginning it was a large rowing boat which could carry men and horses across this great lake. This was known as the Great Boat and was later joined by the Little Boat which was used to carry smaller loads. These rowing boats lasted until 1870 when the first steam ferry arrived. Then, as now, the ferry pulled itself across the water on two large cables stretched across the lake. Since then the ferry has been replaced three times, each time with a bigger and more modern vessel. Today, although the advent of cars makes the ferry almost unnecessary, it remains a busy and popular way of travelling from one side of the lake to the other and queues of traffic are often found waiting for the ferry. Have no fear though, there is always room for foot passengers and you should not have to wait long for the ferry to return.

Here comes the ferry!

Crossing the lake you can still admire its serene beauty despite the number of other boats on the water. Windermere has provided many things to many people throughout its history. To many it has provided a house, to many others it has provided a place to escape to and enjoy for its peace and beauty. Today it provides North West Water with extra supplies of water during times of high demand and during the war it provided food for the people in the form of perch which were caught and tinned for the home-front.

From the ferry you will get a clear view of Belle Isle, the largest island in the lake and the only island to be currently inhabited. It was in the 15th century that Walter de Lindesay first took up residence on the island which has had many owners ever since. In 1774 the then owner, Mr English, had a house specially designed and built on the island. This cylindrical house with its dome and lantern can still be seen on the island which now belongs to the Curwen family. Mr English sold the house and island to the Curwens for the bargain price of £1,700 not long after the house had been completed. Apparently his friends ridiculed the design of this new house. The first of the Curwens to live on the island was Isabel Curwen after whom the island is named. The view from the middle of the lake is also another of West's viewpoints – so out with your landscape mirrors!

On reaching the eastern shore of Windermere walk up the road for 300 yards to a public footpath sign for Bowness on the left. Turn left by the sign, walk across a car park and continue on the clear path between the railings. Cross the field to a road. Cross the road and walk up the lane opposite between the pitch and putt and the cemetery. This leads to the steamer piers at the heart of Bowness.

TOUR DAY 6:
BOWNESS-ON-WINDERMERE

Accommodation

It would seem that every other building in Bowness is either a gift shop or a B&B such is Bowness' relationship with the tourist. The town has accommodation in abundance of every size and price. So much so that Windermere and Bowness take up nearly half of the local council's Where To Stay booklet on their own. Having said that, it is possible to find yourself in Bowness without a bed for the night particularly in mid summer when the town is awash with visitors. It is always wise to book in advance. Telephone Bowness Tourist Information Centre on (05394) 42895.

BOWNESS

If the Lake District as a whole is a honey pot, then Bowness is surely the largest jar in the cupboard. It attracts visitors of every sort, both day trippers and holiday makers, both young and old. On Bank Holidays and in the summer you can find yourself fighting your way through a jungle of people almost wishing you had a machete to make progress easier. But the crowds must come for a reason and indeed Bowness still retains a beauty and charm that people are drawn to. Because of this people either loath it or love it. Ruskin for instance, even a hundred years ago, called the tourists "stupid herds who let themselves be emptied like coals from a sack at Windermere". On the other hand Jessica Lofthouse, a great travel writer, describes Bowness as "a pleasant spot full of happy people when the sun shines...so that only the most unsociable among us could decry it".

Bowness-on-Windermere, as it should really be called, began life as a small village in the 10th century. At this time a Viking chief called Vinand called the large lake after himself 'Vinand's Mere' whilst the village name comes from the Norse for Bull's Headland. As trade increased, particularly between the two great wool towns of Hawkshead

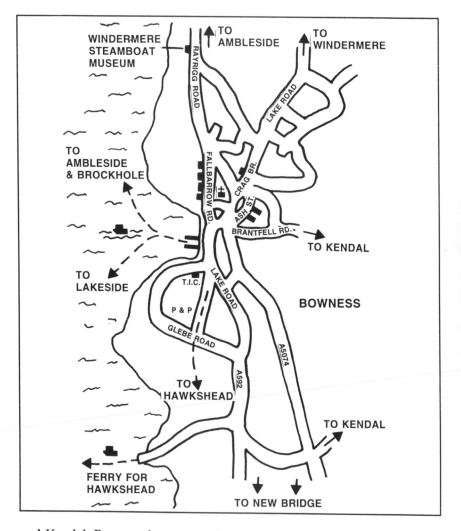

and Kendal, Bowness became an important stopping point for travellers crossing on the ferry. The town therefore contains several old inns which now provide accommodation for travellers of a different kind. It was the arrival of these new travellers or tourists, which really saw the growth of Bowness. During the Victorian period it was fashionable to come to Bowness and hire a boat on the water much as it still is today. The early boatmen who hired out the boats, invented a magical creature called the

Tizzie Wizzie which they claimed could be found under the piers at dusk. In this way they encouraged Victorian gentlemen to hire their boats and take their ladies under the pier for a spot of hunting! I'm sure the gentlemen needed little encouragement. A rare specimen of a real Tizzie Wizzie can still be seen at the Tourist Information Centre in Bowness.

The first public steamer on Windermere ran from Bowness in 1845. Three years later the arrival of the train at nearby Birthwaite meant an influx of tourists from which Bowness has never looked back (or recovered from, depending on your point of view). Birthwaite grew and became Windermere, named after the station from which the tourists alighted to visit the lake. This is possibly the only known case of a town being named after a station rather than the other way around. The two towns of Bowness and Windermere have now grown to such an extent that it is difficult to see where one stops and the other starts.

This new found popularity during the Victorian age also attracted new residents to the area. The new rich industrialists from Lancashire with

Bowness Bay

money to spend and a taste for extravagance built several large houses along the eastern shore of Windermere. One of these is now the Belsfield Hotel which overlooks Bowness pier. This was once the home of H.W. Schneider, the wealthy Furness steel and ship magnate. To reach his offices at Barrow he would walk down to the pier each morning to his private steam launch, *The Esperance,* followed by his butler carrying his breakfast. He would breakfast on the launch which would take him to Lakeside from where he caught the train to Barrow.

Bowness, of course, remains very much a tourist town geared towards the visitor, particularly the day trippers who arrive by the coachload from all over the country. For this reason the town has the feel of a seaside prom about it with ice cream, fudge and gift shops of every kind. It still manages to retain a certain dignity, however, and has not yet lowered itself to the demands of some tourists who ask where the bingo is. Hidden amongst the array of shops there are still some delights such as St. Martin's Church and various museums and exhibitions which are worth a visit. Bowness has much to offer, more than first sight would lead us to believe. This is something many day trippers should bear in mind before heading towards the Information Centre to ask the apparently common question, "Excuse me, where is the National Park?".

ST. MARTIN'S CHURCH

St. Martin's Church stands in the middle of Bowness, somewhat lost amongst the shops and pubs which surround it. The present church was built around 1480 after a much earlier building was destroyed by fire and it is the oldest building in Bowness. The font inside the church together with some of the stained glass windows are thought to have survived from the original church. The East Window in particular is a fine example of an early stained glass window and was in fact taken from Cartmel Priory. In the window can be seen the area's connection with America in the form of a coat of arms. In the pane near the top of the third light from the right you will see the coat of arms of John Washington (1403) who was the 12th ancestor of the famous George Washington. If you dig out your binoculers you will even see the stars and stripes displayed on the shield. The church also contains an ancient wood carving of its patron saint, Martin.

Outside in the churchyard is a much sadder memorial. Here lies the common grave of 47 people who were drowned in 1635 when the ferry across Windermere capsized. The victims were members of a large wedding party returning from Hawkshead at dusk on the 19th October. Over 50 people and 8 horses crammed onto the large rowing boat and it is hardly surprising when the boat sank with a terrible loss of life.

WINDERMERE STEAMBOAT MUSEUM

Windermere Steamboat Museum is probably the best collection of steamboats in the world. It contains many of the Victorian and Edwardian steam launches and yachts which once ploughed up and down the lake. There is *The Lady Elizabeth,* a small steamboat once used by anglers; there is *The Dolly,* the oldest propeller-driven steamboat in the world; *The Raven,* a small cargo ship which once delivered supplies to Windermere's lakeside houses; and the great iron steam yacht, *The Esperance,* which once belonged to the industrialist H.W. Schneider. All these and many others are maintained by the Museum in full working order and pristine condition, making the whole place look rather like a Victorian showroom for boats. All the boats are displayed afloat, though most are under cover so you can examine the boats at your leisure whatever the weather. If the weather is fine, then the museum runs daily cruises on one of its launches, *The Osprey,* for museum visitors. This gives you the chance to cruise the lake like a true Victorian gentleman or lady.

As well as these beautiful and elegant steamboats, the Museum also contains early examples of motorboats from the 1920s and 1930s as well as vintage canoes and sailboats, including Arthur Ransome's *Amazon.*

If you should tire of looking at boats then the Museum includes a photographic display illustrating the history of the lake and the boats which have sailed upon it. There is also a refreshment kiosk but if you wish to eat your own food, the lakeside setting provides a perfect picnic site.

Getting There: The Windermere Steamboat Museum is to be found on Rayrigg Road some quarter of a mile from the Bowness piers (see map).

Opening Times: The museum is open every day from Easter to the end of October from 10.00 a.m. to 5.00 p.m.. Tel. (05394) 45565.

Admission: The entrance price is reasonable (band A) with discounts for family groups.

THE OLD LAUNDRY

The Old Laundry Centre on Crag Brow in the centre of Bowness is a relatively new exhibition and visitors' centre featuring various activities and displays throughout the year. Firstly, it is home to the World of Beatrix Potter which takes you on a fantastic journey through the world of this famous author. Many of her characters are brought to life in the form of 3D displays and you can wander through Mr. McGregor's potting shed or nosey around Mrs Tiggie-winkle's cave. Video walls, film and special effects combine to bring the stories to life.

The centre also contains an exhibition area and a 300 seat theatre. Within these it holds such events as antiques fairs, craft shows, photographic and painting exhibitions as well as various talks and presentations on the Lakes. During the summer months the Centre's theatre plays host to a range of productions from a touring theatre company.

Although the Beatrix Potter exhibition is really of interest only to fans of the author or children, the centre's fine range of events caters for most other people and it is always worth checking the latest events leaflet or 'phoning to ask what is going on. Tel. (05394) 88444.

Opening Times: The Centre is open all year, every day except Christmas and New Year. It opens at 10.00 a.m. and closes at 8.00 p.m. between Easter and October and at 4.00 p.m. the rest of the year.

Admission: Admission to the World of Beatrix Potter is relatively cheap (band A). The cost of the other activities range from band A upwards, depending on the event.

BOATING

The most popular pastime in Bowness (with perhaps the exception of shopping) is to take to the water in a boat. It seems that during the season the world and his wife are afloat on Windermere in some sort of vessel and the lake's surface is dotted with boats of all sizes.

Still the most popular is to hire a rowing boat or small motor boat from Bowness pier. Although you will no longer find any Tizzie Wizzies lurking beneath the piers, it is still a pleasant way to pass an hour or so, rowing out across the lake, perhaps even taking a picnic on the opposite shore. These boats are definitely the most traditional and relaxed way of seeing the lake, particularly if you get someone else to do the rowing.

If the silent grace of the sailing-boat is more your style then Windermere has two sailing centres based near Bowness.

Windermere Sailing Centre: Found on Rayrigg Road, this centre provides equipment and courses in sailing, windsurfing and canoeing. So whether a beginner or more experienced you can take to the lake in your own little craft. The centre is open from March to October every day until dusk. The prices vary according to the activity, the duration and whether you need tution, but prices are generally reasonable (band C upwards). Tel. (05394) 88107 for details.

Lakeland Sailing Ltd.: This company provide sailing for those who require more luxury and less work. Based at the Ferry Nab, they offer day and weekend courses on their luxury 30 foot plus, sailing yachts. Here you can cruise the waters in style, learn how to sail these beautiful craft and even be given lunch on board. However, this does not come cheap and prices are pretty heady (band F). The centre is open all year. Tel. (05394) 46511/2/3 for more information.

There is, of course, always the passenger ferries if all this is a little too energetic. You already know about the rise of the iron steamships on Windermere from the day in Newby Bridge and these magnificent ships arrive here every 30 minutes as they make their way along the lake. However, here at Bowness the great iron ships have competition from the Bowness Bay Boating Company who run smaller launches between Bowness and Ambleside as well as trips around the islands. Their familiar blue boats run every half hour from Bowness and the fare is slightly cheaper than their bigger rivals. For more information contact:

Iron Steamboat Company, Lakeside Pier. Tel. (05395) 31188 or
Bowness Bay Boating Company, Bowness Pier. Tel. (05394) 43360.

The Bowness Bay Boating Company operates all year and because it uses
smaller vessels has the added advantage of being able to do request
stops at Brockhole, The National Park Visitor's Centre.

BROCKHOLE

Brockhole is a fine whitewashed and colonnade house, standing proudly
on the eastern shore of Windermere between Ambleside and Bowness. It
was built in 1899 for another wealthy industrialist, William Henry
Gaddum from Manchester. The house itself was designed by a young
architest, Daniel Gibson, whilst the splendid gardens were laid out by a
famous landscape gardener of the time, Thomas Mawson.

The property later became a nursing home before being bought by the
Lake District Special Planning Board in 1966 who turned it into the
country's first and only National Park Visitor's Centre. Today you can
tour the house and gardens and discover, not only about the house itself,
but about the Lake District National Park. Inside the house you will find
exhibitions which tell the story of the Park and the area – how the lakes
were formed millions of years ago, the influence of man and how the
National Park came into being. These include sections on geology,
natural history and literature. You will also find a lecture room where
local experts give daily talks on a whole range of subjects. There is also a
gift shop as well as Gaddums Restaurant and Tearooms.

Outside, there is just as much going on. The gardens are laid out much
as they were when Thomas Mawson first planned them and with the
help of Sir Michael Holden playing the part of Mawson, you are able to
take an audio tour of the grounds. There is an adventure playground for
the children as well as putting and croquet greens. You can follow the
extensive nature trail around the grounds or even have a go at dry stone
walling in one corner of the garden.

The best thing about Brockhole, however, is that there is always
something happening. Whatever day of the year it is, whenever
Brockhole is open an event is guaranteed. This may be a guided walk
with a Park Ranger, a course on water-colour painting, a session on

botanical medicine, a theatre production in the grounds, a teddy bears' picnic, building bird boxes, creating a badger's sett, courses on map reading, a cycle festival, a lesson in hedge laying or much, much more. All these activities and events are advertised at the beginning of the season in the Park's Events booklet available from Tourist Information Centres throughout the Lakes. So you are able to check beforehand which event appeals and plan your trip accordingly. A visit to Brockhole on the boat from Bowness could easily fill a whole day and is an ideal way to escape the hustle and bustle of Bowness town.

Getting There: There are two ways of getting to Brockhole from Bowness. As already mentioned, you can take one of the boats of the Bowness Bay Boating Company which run regularly from Bowness Pier.

Alternatively you could travel on one of the many buses which run from Bowness Pier including, if you can brave the weather, an open top bus.

Opening Times: Brockhole is open from April to November every day, 10.00 a.m. to 5.00 p.m. Tel. (05394) 46601 for details.

Admission: In 1992 admision to Brockhole was free for the first time and I hope this will continue. You will, of course, have to pay for any courses or events you take part in, but these are all relatively cheap (band A or B).

OTHER ATTRACTIONS

Bowness is very much geared towards the tourist and in particular the day tripper. For this reason it has many other attractions which require no great discription and are listed below.

Countryside Theatre: Situated next to the Tourist Information Centre on Glebe Road, this small theatre is owned by the National Park who run daily talks, lectures and films on the environment and history of the Lakes. All the talks are given by local experts and Rangers and are extremely interesting. An ideal pastime for those all too often rainy days.

Lake Windermere Aquarium: Also on Glebe Road, this small and slightly unusual enterprise displays an interesting array of freshwater fish which are to be found in Windermere, including the famous char. There is also a small shop.

Royality Cinema: For those who want to spend an evening on the back row catching the latest releases, Bowness has its very own cinema. This can be found on Lake Road.

Pitch and Putt: If you are a golf enthusiast who is suffering withdrawal symptoms for your local links or if you just wish to embarrass your husband on the greens, then Bowness has a small pitch and putt course. Armed with a putter and a 5 iron you can pretend to be Nick Faldo for the afternoon. The course is to be found on Rectory Road.

Mountain Bike Hire: If your desire is to take to the hills on two wheels then there are a couple of cycle hire shops in the area, one in Bowness itself and the other at Windermere, right next to the station. This is presumably to catch the tourists as they get off the train!

Windermere Cycle Centre, West View Galley, South Terrace, Bowness. Tel. (05394) 44479.

Lakeland Leisure, The Chalet, Station Precinct, Windermere. Tel. (05394) 44786.

WALK DAY 7:
BOWNESS TO KENDAL

Route: Bowness – Lindeth – Gilpin Mill – St. Catherine's Church – Capplerigg – Cunswick Scar – Kendal.

Distance: 10 miles.

Maps: 1:50,000 O.S. Landranger No. 97 Kendal to Morecambe or 1:25,000 O.S. Outdoor Leisure English Lakes S.E.

Getting There: The start of the walk at Bowness is probably the most accessible of all the starts apart from Kendal itself. It is just a 15 minute bus ride from Windermere station with regular buses between the two.

By car follow the A591 from junction 36 of the M6 until you reach Windermere. Here you should turn left opposite the Windermere Hotel following the signs for the lake. Bowness is $1^1/_2$ miles from Windermere.

The Walk

There are many routes which link Bowness and Kendal, amongst them the Dales Way. However, instead of using this well used route I have headed southwards joining a string of farms together along old rights of way and wonderful pack-horse routes. Out of all the walks on the Trail, this stands out as one of my favourites. The paths are old and little used and we didn't meet a soul all day, but at the same time they are clear, easy to follow and a delight to walk. In contrast to the rest of the Trail there is little woodland and the scenery is much more pastoral. Towards the end of the walk we follow one of the best, yet relatively unknown, pack-horse routes, Capplerigg Lane. The day finishes with a short climb up Cunswick Scar – a smaller version of its neighbour, Scout Scar – to end the walk as we started it all those days ago.

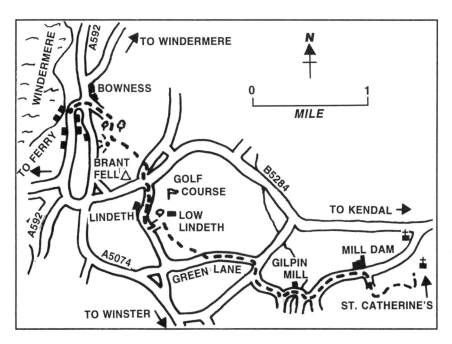

Section 1: Bowness to St. Catherine's Church

Starting from the pier in Bowness follow the main road into the town, bearing right up St. Michael's Hill. Here turn left up Brantfell Road. Follow the road for quarter of a mile to its end. Go through the metal gate and continue on the grass track.

Here there is a sign on the gatepost for Ilkley 81 miles. This is for the Dales Way walkers since this is also the start of the Dales Way. We will quickly leave the Dales Way behind and make our own way to Kendal.

After the first kissing gate turn right on the track through the beech and yew woods to another wooden kissing gate. Go through the gate and follow the path ahead to the viewpoint.

This stunning viewpoint, though only a few minutes walk from Bowness, is rarely visited by the hordes of tourists who instead prefer to wander the streets below you. In fact, you are more likely to meet locals up here than tourists.

Turning your back on the lake follow the path to the ladder stile ahead. Go over the stile and follow the fence on your left to pass behind the farm. (Ignore the yellow arrows which take you on a small diversion to the top of Brant Fell.) After the farm follow the track which leads to a tarmac lane. Turn right and follow the lane to a crossroads. Here head straight across and down the lane opposite (Lindeth Lane) following the signs for Winster. Continue on the lane for quarter of a mile, past the golf course and Lindeth Farm to the next farm track on the left for Low Lindeth. Turn left across the cattle grid and follow the tarmac track for 20 yards. Here turn off the track to the right, heading to the right of a small knoll, to cross the field to the corner of a wall. From here follow an indistinct path parallel with the wall on your right to a ladder stile on the opposite side of the field. Cross the ladder stile and follow the path straight ahead through the bracken. The path becomes less clear and intermittent but if you keep heading slightly right you will come to a metal gate onto a walled track on the opposite side of the plantation.

As you navigate your way through these stunted trees and bracken you may notice other, smaller plants amongst the grass. One of the most abundant is the small, white flower of the eyebright. Like the lousewort, this small plant is semi-parasitic with suckered roots which attach to nearby hosts. However, it still relies on insects for pollination and its tiny, white flowers are streaked with yellow and violet lines which act as 'honey guides' directing the small flies to the centre of the flower. To early herbalists, these yellow and purple markings resembled a bloodshot eye. The trend at the time was the Doctrine of Signatures which decreed that all plants were stamped with a physical sign of their medical properties. They therefore believed that this plant must be a cure for tired and damaged eyes. In fact Culpepper says of the plant "If the herb was as much used as neglected, it would spoil half the spectacle makers' trade". This is, of course, how the plant gets its name and in this case the unfounded belief has actually proved to be right. Today eyebright is still used as an excellent remedy for sore, itchy eyes as either a compress or eyewash.

At the gate go onto the track and turn left. Follow this green lane for half a mile to the road. This old, green lane runs downhill between two walls as a remnant of the many green lanes and pack-horse routes which once criss-crossed this area. The main ones were made into turnpike roads and were eventually tarmacked and widened. Today this lane survives as a rocky track across the fields.

The edge of the track is lined with another plant which has a fascinating history, broom. Its curious name comes from the fact that the long, flexible stems make an excellent besom and it is still used in some parts of the country for this purpose. Its old Latin name, however, has played an important part in England's Royal history.

In the early 12th century it was a common superstition that the flowers and seed pods of broom would bring luck to its wearer and save them from harm. Because of this Geoffery of Anjou, an important man of the day, would wear a sprig of broom in his hat when going into battle. His son, Henry, also took to wearing a sprig of the plant and in 1154 when Henry became Henry II of England he took the Latin name of broom, *Planta Genista*, as his family name. Thus the Plantagenet family was born and ruled over England for many generations.

On the road turn right to a junction after 200 yards. Here turn left and follow the lane down into the valley bottom, following the sign for Crossthwaite. At the bottom of the hill the lane crosses a stream at Gilpin Mill before starting to climb the opposite side of the valley. At the next two junctions turn left then follow the lane for quarter of a mile to a farm and white fence on the left.

Strolling along this leafy lane you may notice that many of the leaves bear small, black spots. In late summer many of the trees, particularly the sycamore, seem almost to have an arboreal plague of measles. We can lay the blame for this outbreak firmly at the feet of the aphid (all six of them). The gardener's enemy, this little sap-sucker taps into the leaf's transport system and syphons off the sugary sap. Now sap is not a particularly good food source and your dentist would certainly not recommend it since it is high in sugar but low in everything else. The poor, little aphid has to eat vast quantities of the stuff just to get what it needs. The stuff it doesn't need, mostly sugars, are passed out at the back of the aphid in a fluid called honeydew. When you park your car under a tree in summer and you return to find the window screen covered in small specks of gooey liquid, that's honeydew. When the aphids are not excreting onto your car they are doing it onto the leaves which soon become covered in this sugary liquid. This is an ideal place for fungus to grow and hence the black dots which cover the leaves.

All that is left of St Catherine's Church

At the farm, turn right down a small lane and follow this for 400 yards to the second cattle grid. Turn left in front of the grid through a wooden gate and follow the bridleway by the wall on your left. Continue on the bridleway (ignoring the public footpath sign off to the right) for 300 yards to a gate. Go through the gate and straight ahead until you are by an old hedge on your left. Follow this hedge, then along a short length of track to a wooden gate. Do not go through the gate but turn left in front of the gate to the corner of the field and a gap in the wall. Go through the gap and bear right, around the outcrop of rock to the remains of St. Catherine's Church.

Section 2: St. Catherine's Church to Kendal

Once the church of Crook and now a crooked church, all that remains of St. Catherine's is the crumbling tower and the old graveyard wall. The rest of the building has disappeared and even the tower is unsafe to explore. However, the setting is pleasant enough and it makes an ideal spot to rest and have lunch under the shade of the old church yews.

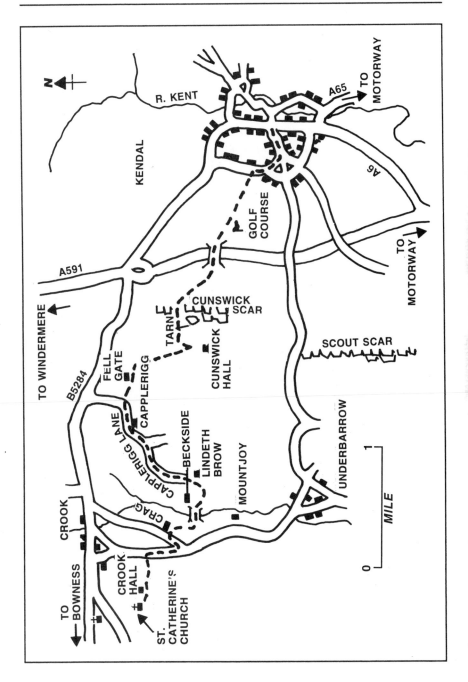

Facing south with your back to the church, go through the gate to your left to follow the clear track to the farmyard and Crook Hall. Pass through the yard and along the track on the other side to, and over, a cattle grid. Continue on the track for 350 yards until it meets another track. Bear left on this new track to a lane.

Turn right on the lane and continue for 400 yards to a junction. Turn left and continue for 100 yards to a farm and a public footpath sign for Low Crag Farm. Turn right to follow the sign down a track to a kissing gate. After the gate, follow the wall on your right to a gap in the wall. Go through the gap and now with the wall on your left, continue across two fields to a farm track. Turn left and follow the track to Beckside Farm.

The next farm south of you from here is Mountjoy, once the home of Miles Bateman, one of George Fox's Valiant Sixty. Under the influence of Fox, he left his home to travel the country preaching and teaching the new Quaker religion. He was away from home so much that his wife once complained "Would to God I had married a drunkard. Then I might have found him in the alehouse, but now I cannot tell where to find my husband".

The track to Beckside Farm leads over a beautifully picturesque stone bridge across a stream which spreads out into a small pool at this point. Here some beautiful wetland flowers grow in the flooded grass, amongst them the aromatic water mint. Water mint has a strong but cool, minty smell which can be used to relax and relieve tired limbs when scattered into a hot bath. However, when crossed with the sharper smelling spearmint the result is the hot, strong peppermint, still grown commercially to supply the peppermint cream makers.

Walk through the farmyard and out through a metal gate at the far end. Follow the track on the other side of the gate to another gate and cattle grid. Continue on the track, which bears left and across the field to pass a derelict building on the far side. At the cattle grid the track meets another track. Turn left along this new track which runs between two stone walls.

This is Capplerigg Lane, probably the best, neatest and greenest pack-horse route in the country. The grass under your feet looks almost mowed in places and is a delight to walk on. The fact that the lane is so long is also unusual and over the next mile or so, we can get some idea of what travelling was like in the past when all roads were like this.

Continue on the green lane for half a mile to a junction of lanes and a public bridleway sign. Here turn left and continue past the farm after 300 yards, through a metal gate and onto a tarmac lane. Turn left along the lane to a wooden gate on your right after 30 yards. Go through this gate and turn right to a ladder stile. Cross the stile and turn left across the field to the next ladder stile. Go over the stile, then follow the wall on your right to a lane into Fell Gate Farm. In the farmyard turn left before the barn and out on a track between electric fences. Continue on the track as it leads through a metal gate and bears right to the diagonally opposite corner of the field. Pass through a gateway, then left through a gate into another field. Head for the diagonally opposite corner of this long, thin field.

Off to your left you will have already spotted a small, wooded 'cliff'. This is Cunswick Scar, a small extension of Scout Scar. We are slowly heading for this escarpment and shall soon be climbing its wooded slopes. Meanwhile if you look around this field you may spot the occasional sorrel plant. This common, narrow leaved dock is making something of a come-back in culinary circles and the upmarket nouvelle cuisine chefs have discovered the wonderful bitter, lemony taste of this country vegetable. Used in salads, sauces and stews since medieval times, this versatile herb is more widely used in France where it is used as the main ingredient in a delicious soup.

Just before you reach the corner of the field, you will find a stile on your left. Cross this into the next field then turn right to follow the fence on your right to a path which leads uphill through the trees on your left. Follow the path through the trees then by another electric fence to a stile over the fence. Cross the stile (carefully!) and cross the lane to a track by the wall. Turn left to follow the track with the wall on your right for quarter of a mile to a metal bar stile in the wall. Turn right over the stile and into the woods. Follow the path through the woods and then into a field. Head straight across the field to a gate opposite. Pass through the gate and into the woods then go right, along the edge of the woods to a stile. Go over this stile and take the path to the left which leads uphill through the trees.

This is the side of Cunswick Scar and the woods here lie virtually undisturbed and full of wildlife. When we passed this way in early Autumn, there were dozens of mushrooms of various size, colour and edibility. The path comes out of the woods through a kissing gate at the top of the Scar.

The top of Cunswick Scar is said to be haunted by the ghost of one of the Legburne family who once lived at Cunswick Hall. They were apparently a wild family who performed strange rituals on their land, although they did allow Henry VIII to use Cunswick Hall as a trysting place when he was courting Catherine Parr. Which of the Legburnes' spirits roams this hill and for what reason is unknown.

On the top of Cunswick Scar walk straight ahead, away from the edge, to meet a wall on your right. Follow this wall to a metal bar stile in the wall itself. Cross the stile and follow the clear path across the field to a footbridge over the dual-carriageway. Cross the bridge then walk straight ahead to a gap in the wall. Go through the gap and follow the wall on your left to and through the next gap onto Kendal Golf Course. Continue by the wall on your left for 200 yards to where the wall bears off to the left. Here follow the path ahead over a small wall and along a clear path. This leads downhill to a wall at the bottom of the hill. Turn right by the wall and follow it to a gateway. Continue through the gateway along the path which becomes a tarmac lane and leads downhill onto Serpentine Road. Turn right and follow the road to a T-junction with Beast Banks, which you once climbed at the start of the walk. Turn left and return downhill to the starting point of the Trail at Kendal Tourist Information Centre.

Well done! You have completed this 73 mile circuit of South Lakeland and finished the Furness Trail. I hope you feel a little tired but very pleased with yourself, as you surely should. After all, what is the point of completing a long distance walk if you cannot indulge in a little self pride. Now the hard work is over though, it would surely be a pity if you simply loaded your bags and headed home without spending a day exploring the best town on the Trail. So tarry a while in this 'ould grey town' and bask in its character and your own glory.

Finishing the Trail into Kendal!

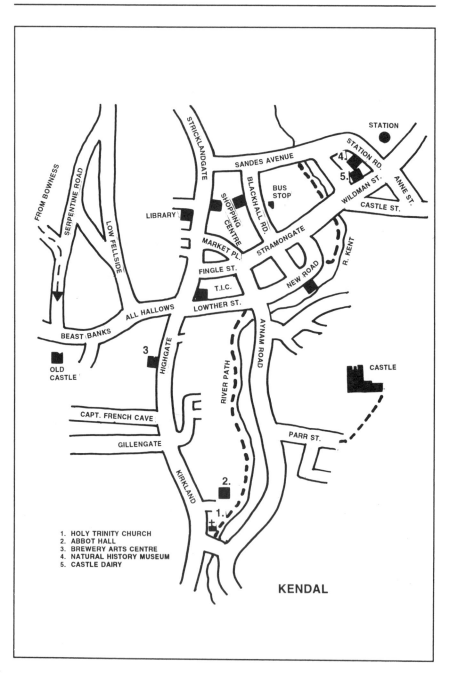

STATION

STRICKLANDGATE

STATION RD.

SANDES AVENUE

4.

FROM BOWNESS

SERPENTINE ROAD

LOW FELLSIDE

BLACKHALL RD.

BUS
STOP

5.

WILDMAN ST.

ANNE ST.

LIBRARY

SHOPPING CENTRE

CASTLE ST.

MARKET PL.

STRAMONGATE

R. KENT

FINGLE ST.

NEW ROAD

ALL HALLOWS

T.I.C.

LOWTHER ST.

BEAST BANKS

3

HIGHGATE

AYNAM ROAD

CASTLE

OLD
CASTLE

RIVER PATH

CAPT. FRENCH CAVE

GILLENGATE

PARR ST.

KIRKLAND

2.

1.

1. HOLY TRINITY CHURCH
2. ABBOT HALL
3. BREWERY ARTS CENTRE
4. NATURAL HISTORY MUSEUM
5. CASTLE DAIRY

KENDAL

TOUR DAY 7: KENDAL

Accommodation

Although not as popular as say Bowness, Kendal nevertheless owes much of its current prosperity to tourists and there are many bed and breakfasts, guest houses and hotels of every kind. Most of these are situated in or around the town centre and you won't have to look hard to find somewhere to stay. If you wish to book somewhere in advance then ring Kendal Tourist Information Centre on (0539) 725758.

KENDAL

The best way to see Kendal is from the castle. If you cross the river and climb the steep hill to the stone ruins, the view from here allows you to

Kendal's Market Place

see the town laid out before you like some Lego-built toy town. If anyone did decide to build a replica of Kendal from Lego, they would need only grey and white bricks since the houses, shops and offices seem carved from the very rock itself. In some ways they are, for most of the buildings are built from the grey limestone on which the town stands.

Kendal's name comes from the name of the river which flows through its heart, the Kent. Kent-dale once applied to the valley as a whole and the town was called Kirkby Kendal, 'the church town of Kent Dale'. Over time the Kirkby was lost and the town became simply Kendal.

Kendal grew because of its position. Lying on the main fording points of the River Kent it has been a junction of important trade routes even before the Romans arrived. When the Romans did come they built a fort, *Alavana*, on one of the main fording points which lies to the south of the present town. This fort would have been a strategic link in the Roman road between Lancaster and Ravenglass. The Anglo-Saxons chose a second fording point, further upstream, to build their settlement and in the 8th century erected a cross and small church. This became Kirkland and the present town of Kendal developed around this point.

As you know from the first chapter, the first castle to be built in Kendal was in 1092 and was later replaced by a stone castle. This stone castle was said to have been built after a terrible massacre of the Kendal people by the Scottish raiders in 1189. During the raid the Scots even killed all who had taken refuge in the church. Many say that much of the town's present layout is due to the marauding Scots. It is believed that Kendal's famous yards, which lie along the main street, were built for defence. A group of houses and shops built around a small yard with a narrow entrance onto the main street, they could be shut up tight and easily defended against attackers. However, other authors point out that the yards were constructed long after the Scots had become benign and that they were actually built to cram many people into a small space. Either way, the tiny alleys and courtyards provide excellent exploration for the inquisitive, with nooks and crannies in abundance.

Another conspicuous feature of Kendal's main street is the number of pubs and inns. This is a throw-back to Kendal's importance as a trading post and pack-horse station. Before the turnpike roads were built and all goods were transported by pack-horse, 350 pack-horses would make their way through Kendal every week. The many pubs and inns would provide stable and accommodation for horse and driver. During this time Kendal was the most important pack-horse station between Wigan and Scotland.

The names of the pubs reflect the pack-horses' cargo. The two main inns on Stricklandgate are The Woolpack and The Fleece, for the horses carried mainly wool. Wool was, for a long time, Kendal's prosperity and the town's motto, *Pannus Mihi Panis* or Wool is my Bread, speaks for itself. Surrounded by the largest sheep runs in Europe, including the wool producing area around Hawkshead, medieval Kendal made its fortune producing coarse woollen cloth worn by the working men and women of Elizabethan England. Many of the old cottages in Kendal were built to house hand-loom weavers and when the Industrial Revolution and power driven looms came along, Kendal was ideally placed on the River Kent to build water driven mills. Much of the cloth produced in Kendal was dyed a distinctive green colour using a mixture of woad blue and greenweed yellow. This Kendal Green became known throughout the Kingdom and even gets a mention in Shakespeare's plays. With all this trade and coming and going of travellers, it is hardly surprising that Kendal became a market town and its charter was granted in 1189, the first in Cumbria. A thriving market still exists in Kendal on Wednesdays and Saturdays when stalls spill from the Market Place, off the main street, down the hill and along Stramongate.

Kendal did not produce just woollen cloth, but diversified into stockings and carpets as well as some local gunpowder and bobbin production. This served the town well when, in the 17th century, Westmorland cloth and Kendal Green lost its popularity and the wool trade went into decline. Kendal fought back for a while by exporting the rough cloth to the tobacco plantations of America. Here the owners were not concerned with what the black slaves wore as long as it was cheap. In return Kendal imported tobacco to produce snuff and became a major snuff producer. Indeed, if you take a walk down Lowther Street you can still spot the turbaned Turk with his box of snuff hanging from the wall and still catch the strong odour of snuff as you pass by.

Today the cloth weavers and stocking makers of Kendal have all disappeared. After the decline in the wool trade in the 17th and 18th century the town stopped growing and although the building of the

Lancaster Canal in 1819 provided a short-lived life line, the subsequent decline of the canal and the building of the railway line outside of the town, meant that Kendal never really recovered its great history and importance. This does not mean that the town itself declined. No, instead it diversified and today Kendal has the K-Shoes factory and Provincial Insurance together with many other small firms to keep the locals in employment. This self-sufficiency of the town and its people has meant the town has not succumbed to the trappings of tourism and though popular with visitors it has not lined its streets with gift shops and tea rooms. Instead its main street and new shopping centre provide a pleasant mix of shops providing for both locals and visitors alike. The buildings themselves also provide a pleasant mix of architectural style and age, reflecting Kendal's history and changing fortunes. For these reasons it is an interesting and fun town to explore. There are many town-trails produced by various historians and authors which are available at the Tourist Information Centre and provide details on each building. Alternatively you can wander at will around Kendal since you don't really need to know about the history or age of a particular building to enjoy the atmosphere and charm of this beautiful town. For those who are interested, I have given a little information on the most obvious buildings in the town such as the church, the castle, etc.

For me Kendal is, and always will be, a favourite. I adore its shops, its people, its lively market and the cosiness it seems to create. Maybe this is because it always rains when I go there, or maybe its because my favourite restaurant is there, or maybe its because I am familiar with its idiosyncrasies. Or maybe, just maybe, its because I got married there (I know, call me an old romantic).

HOLY TRINITY CHURCH

The parish church of Kendal lies between the main road and the river at the southern end of the town. 103 feet wide, with four aisles and an 80 foot tower, the Holy Trinity Church is said to be the largest parish church in England. It certainly strikes an impressive sight, set in a small park of trees and lawns by the river and, when its peal of ten bells start ringing, an impressive sound as well. The Church owes its great size to its longevity and the various wealthy families who have added or improved on the original building.

There has been a cross and church on this site since the 8th century and part of this original cross can still be seen within the present Church. The church itself was first mentioned in the Doomsday Book of 1080. This church was rebuilt by Ivo de Talebois in 1087. By 1201 there was a chancel, a nave, two aisles and a tower. During the following century the Church was rebuilt again. The tower was replaced and the nave and aisles extended to give the Church a wider four aisles, the inner two once part of the original structure. Between the 14th and 16th centuries the Parrs, Stricklands and Bellinghams all added their own private chapels to the building, extending the Church further still. After a Victorian re-vamp of the Church we have the present building.

The inside contains many features depicting its history and importance. You can see the prayer book of Catherine Parr, Kendal's most famous daughter and one time Queen of England. In the Parr chapel itself can be seen Lady Catherine's badge, a maiden's head, carved in the stone above the arched windows. Along the north wall are various brass plates together with the Bellingham Brass showing Sir Roger Bellingham in his armour, his wife in gown and cape and his pet dog curled at their feet. The Church supplies materials and instructions for you to take your own brass rubbings of these magnificence plates. Also on display are the colours of the King's Own Royal Border Regiment as well as the military hardware of Robin the Devil. Robin the Devil of Crook was a local Royalist during the Civil War who rode into Kendal Church looking for Roundheads. Cromwell's supporters had already gone and after killing a townsman who had tried to stop him entering the Church, he rode off but not before he had lost his helmet and sword in the fracas. This, together with the massacre of 1189, gives the Church a rather macabre history.

Today the building is quiet and peaceful and worthy of exploration. Besides the sights already mentioned you can also see the corona of the 'Apostle of the North' over the altar in memory to Bernard Gilpin as well as a modern 'Crown of Thorns' made of stainless steel in the 1960s and hung over the chancel. The Church also contains a small bookstall.

Outside in the churchyard stands a 19th century replica of the famous Anglo-Saxon cross at Irton. All in all, the Holy Trinity provides welcome relief from the sometimes hectic streets of Kendal and its undoubtable history and imposing structure will please even the most sceptic.

KENDAL CASTLE

From just about everywhere in Kendal you can see what remains of Kendal Castle. Once a great stone fortification and home to the Baron of Kendal, the Castle stands atop a small drumlin which is now a public park.

After Kendal's first castle on the west of the river proved insufficient a larger, stronger stone structure was built by Gilbert Fitz Reinfred at the end of the 12th century. Around this time Kendal was also made a barony by Richard the Lionheart and the Castle became home to the local Baron. The Castle was extended and strengthened in the 13th century and the three towers which can still be seen today were built at this time. In later years the barony of Kendal was split into three parts with the portion including the Castle being given to Sir William Parr. In 1512 his great, great granddaughter, Catherine, was born in the Castle and grew up within its wealthy surroundings. Her father, Sir Thomas, was controller of the King's household and in 1543 Catherine became the sixth wife of Henry VIII, though she herself had been married twice before. Managing to outlive this wife-killing King was quite a feat and she even went on to marry for a fourth time to Admiral Lord Seymour.

The Castle remained in the ownership of the Parrs until the early 17th century, but even as early as 1572 the Castle was reported to be in a decayed state. Over time the structure has fallen into total ruin. Today, if you climb the short but steep path up to the top of the hill on which the Castle stands, you will find the remains of the three towers and an exceptionally thick main wall as well as parts of the curtain wall. This in turn is surrounded by a deep, grassy moat around which you can stroll and imagine Kendal and Castle in its medieval heyday.

CASTLE DAIRY

The Castle Dairy on Wildman Street was built on the site of an earlier dairy in 1566 to serve, as the name suggests, the residents of the nearby Castle. Today it survives as the oldest inhabitable house in Kendal and remains little changed from when it was built. Inside is an array of 16th century architectural features such as a squint window, large inglenooks and a unique Clavey mantelpiece. Much of the previous, earlier dairy can also be seen making up part of the building. For example, the slate kitchen floor is thought to originate from the 12th century.

Upstairs, the main bedroom has a curious barrel-vaulted roof formed of arched oak timbers, specially chosen for their natural curve. The oak bosses between the joists carry the Arms of the Parr and Strickland families and it is said that Catherine herself lived here for a short time. The four poster bed which dominates this room is said to be 500 years old. The carved detail on the head-board is stunning, but for a more human touch look at the floor at the foot of the bed. Here can be seen deep scars carved by the soldiers removing their boots ready for bed.

Like no other building in Kendal, the Castle Dairy provides a taste of life during the town's heyday, with period furniture giving it that lived-in feel.

Opening Times: The Dairy is open from Easter to the end of September on Wednesdays only, from 2.00 p.m. to 4.00 p.m. Tel. (0539) 721170.

Admission: There is a very, very small entrance fee (only 5p in 1992).

ABBOTT HALL- The Museum of Lakeland Life and Industry and the Art Gallery

In 1759 Colonel George Wilson of Milnthorpe had a town residence built for him in Kendal, between the Church and the town centre. At the end of the last century this property was bought by the local council but remained unused until the end of the last war. Since then it has been restored and given a new lease of life as a museum and art gallery.

The house itself holds the Art Gallery. Open in 1962 the building's ground floor has been restored to its original Georgian design and furnished with period furniture. The Gallery also contains other furniture and objet d'art as well as some fascinating paintings. On the walls hang portraits by the local artist, George Romney together with other well known painters. This includes an extensive collection of Lake District water-colours. The Gallery also holds a number of temporary exhibitions which are well worth visiting as is the excellent craft shop which is to be found at the Gallery entrance.

The old stable block of Abbot Hall has been converted into a museum of Lakeland Life, both past and present. This part of the Hall complex was opened in 1971 and attempts to show life as it was in the Lakes through various periods of history. The Museum is fascinating and absorbing with plenty to arouse and stimulate your interest. There is a replica of an 18th century farmhouse kitchen with traditional furniture, griddles over the hearth and other kitchen utensils of the time. There is a Victorian bedroom with a four poster bed and cradle as well as a 1910 Lakeland parlour.

In addition to Lakeland domestic scenes, the Museum portrays the multitude of industries and trades which have been carried out in this small corner of the country. There are, of course, a large number of farm tools and machinery as well as a great number of items from the wool trade from when Kendal was the wool capital of England. Wool combs, spinning wheels, looms and rows of tenterhooks are all on show. The skills of other local craftsmen can also be seen. Blacksmith, wheelwright, clogger, bobbin maker and many more all have their place in the area's rich and diverse history. There is even a display of mechanic's tools surrounding the first ever motorbike to be built in the North West, by Herbet Braithwaite of Stavely in 1912. A reconstructed street scene shows shops of old with the chance to window shop in Marks' Penny Bazaar, Downward's Pharmacy and the local photographer's shop.

Lakeland's literary connections are represented with a copy of Arthur Ransome's study containing many of his personal belongings and a room dedicated to local author John Cunliffe who based his Postman Pat stories in nearby Longsleddale Valley.

The Museum and Gallery provide a glimpse into Lakeland life of the past with period pieces and authentic items of the time and no glass cases to get in the way. A stroll around this complex can easily fill a half day.

Opening Times: The Abbot Hall complex is open all year, every day except Christmas and New Year. The times of opening vary according to the day and the time of year. For most of the year, however, the Hall opens at 10.30 a.m. and closes at 5.00 p.m., except on Sundays when it opens at 2.00 p.m.. Tel. (0539) 722464 for more information.

Admission: The admission price is very reasonable (band A) and well worth the cost.

KENDAL MUSEUM OF NATURAL HISTORY AND ARCHAEOLOGY

Just around the corner from Kendal railway station, this small but crammed museum holds a wonderful series of dioramas entitled 'A Walk Through South Lakeland'. A good chance to re-live the past two weeks? Well, not quite, but it will help you find out more about the geology and natural history of the area you have recently toured. As well as natural history there are displays on local history and the wildlife of the world. Being one of the oldest museums in the country, many of the displays consist of stuffed animals in shocked poses. But don't let this put you off for there is much more to the Museum than this. In particular there is Alfred Wainwright's 'Cabinet of Curiosities' which provides an interesting insight into the great man's thoughts.

Opening Times: Coming under the control of Abbot Hall, the Natural History Museum has the same opening times as the Museum of Lakeland Life and Industry; every Day, all year from 10.30 a.m. to 5.00 p.m. except Sundays. Tel. (0539) 721374 for further details.

Admission: Admission prices are also the same as Abbot Hall (band A).

THE BREWERY ARTS CENTRE

They once brewed beer in Kendal in a large brewery in the centre of town. The beer and brewers have long since gone but the 150 year old brewery still remains, lovingly restored and converted into a small but lively Modern Arts complex. Situated behind the YHA hostel on Highgate, this wonderful building holds many delights. The landscaped gardens at the front contain not only the Centre's famous 'phone box, but also houses temporary sculptures, both weird and wonderful. Inside on the ground floor is a large hall where antique fairs and other events are held. If you make your way up to the gallery, you will find regular exhibitions from various photographers. Next door to the gallery is a small cafe where you can buy a cup of tea or coffee or even a pizza before an evening performance in the theatre. If you require something stronger the cosy bar offers real ale whilst you sit yourself down in one of the Brewery's original cedar vats. I would like to say that the Centre also has a theatre. It once did have and will have again, but at the time of writing they were still in the process of rebuilding it. The Centre does have the Warehouse Gallery though, where many modern artists get to show their interesting and sometimes controversial labour.

The nice thing about the Brewery Arts is that there is always something going on – plays, films, art workshops, music, mime and much more all take place under the Centre's umbrella. Twice a year the Centre dedicates itself to staging special musical festivals. There is the Kendal Jazz Festival held in the autumn and Kendal Folk Festival held in August. At any time, however, the Centre is always worth a visit.

Opening Times: The Centre is open all year, every day except Sundays. It opens at 9.30 a.m. and closes at 6.00 p.m. or later if there is a performance. Check with Kendal Tourist Information Centre or with the Brewery Arts itself for details of events. Tel. (0539) 725133.

Admission: The wonderful thing about the Brewery Arts is that admission to the displays and exhibitions is free. Obviously for films, plays and workshops prices vary.

The Brewery Arts Centre

K-SHOES

Believe it or not, many people come to Kendal with the sole purpose (excuse the pun!) of visiting K-Shoes. K-Shoes have been making footwear in Kendal for many years and the large factory at Netherfield, just south of the town centre, employs a large percentage of Kendal's workforce. The visitors come not to study shoemakers in action but for the big discounts they can get on a whole range of footwear at the factory's shop. Here every type of shoe can be bought from sling-backs to walking boots and should you be in need of a new pair of boots, then it may be worth a visit. The shop also has a snack bar for some light refreshment and to rest your feet!

Opening Times: The factory shop is open all year from Monday to Friday, 10.00 a.m. to 7.00 p.m. and on Saturdays from 9.00 a.m. to 5.00 p.m.

Tel. (0539) 724343 for more information.

EVENTS

Although a calendar of events in the area is included at the end of this book, I could not leave Kendal without mentioning a few of the town's annual activities.

Harness Racing: If you fancy a flutter on the horses, then this is your chance – but with a difference. Horse and sulky racing takes place on an oval, hardstone track at Kendal's County Showground to the north of the town centre. With daytime and evening races throughout the summer, it is possible to enjoy a few hours watching the graceful trot of these harnessed horses as they pull their driver around the track. You might also win a few bob! Tel. Sedbergh (05396) 20113 for times and more details.

Westmorland County Show: Held yearly on the second Thursday in September, this one day event is a celebration of Lakeland life and sports. The Show features agricultural exhibitions of all kinds, though mainly to persuade farmers to use a particular brand of fertilizer. There is, however, many other attractions to interest the visitor. Show-jumping events, sheep dog trials, horse-drawn carriage driving, Cumberland and

Westmorland wrestling and much more. One of Cumbria's best and biggest shows, if you are in Kendal on that day, it's not to be missed. The show is held on the County Showground to the north of the town centre. Contact the Tourist Information Centre in Kendal for more information.

Kendal Gathering: This 17 day gathering is a festival of events and activities covering a wide range of arts and entertainments. There are exhibitions, shows, concerts, dances and many other activities which give you the chance to join in this mini-fiesta. The whole thing ends with the spectacular Torchlight Procession – a carnival of floats and bands marching through Kendal's darkened streets, lit only by torch light. The Kendal Gathering is held in late August/early September to coincide with the County Show. Check with the Tourist Information Centre on dates and events.

Lakeland Rose Show: Once held at Holker Hall, but now transferred to the County Showground in Kendal, this annual show allows top rose-growers from around the country to display the fruits of their labour. However, not just plants are on display here. Car shows, massed bands and parachute displays are all to be seen at this large event. The Rose Show is held on the second weekend in July.

Kendal Folk Festival: Held in late August, this week long programme is organised by the Brewery Arts Centre and includes everything lovers of folk music could wish for. Concerts by both well known and undiscovered folk musicians, workshops for the budding 'folkie' and celidhs to do-sa-do to. Fun for all. Telephone the Brewery Arts for more information.

Kendal Jazz Festival: Usually held in late summer or early autumn, this is a 2 week festival attracting the top names of jazz from around the world. Jazz sessions are held at various venues throughout the town and you cannot go anywhere without hearing the wail of a soulful sax. Telephone the Brewery Arts for further details.

CALENDAR OF EVENTS

During your time on the Trail you will come across many events and festivals which make the walk that more memorable or worthwhile. I often feel that the best discoveries are those made by chance, when you stubble upon a unknown antiques fair or wander into an unpublicised Open Day. However, if you wish to plan your trip around a particular happening then I have put together a calendar of events for the months April to November: Of course, this is by no means a comprehensive list of events but a timetable of regular annual (or biennial) events. Whenever you go to this part of the world you will always find something going on and indeed this is part of its attraction.

I have also supplied a list of Tourist Information Centres for the towns on the Trail so that you can check what else is happening.

APRIL

Kendal Harness Races, County Showground – Start at Easter and occur throughout the summer.

Egg Rolling on Hoad Hill, Ulverston – Easter Monday.

MAY

Cartmel Races, Cartmel – Spring Bank Holiday weekend.

Whit Hiring Fair, The Gill, Ulverston – Whitsun weekend.

JUNE

The Great Garden and Countryside Festival, Holker Hall – 1st weekend in June.

JULY

Lakeland Rose Show, County Showground, Kendal – July weekend.

Barbour Horse Trials, Holker Hall – a middle weekend in July.

Flookburgh Steam Gathering, Flookburgh Airfield – a weekend at the end of July.

Agricultural Show, Bardsea Park, Nr. Ulverston – last Wednesday in July.

AUGUST

Coniston County Fair, Coniston Hall – 1st weekend in August.

Cartmel Show, Cartmel – 1st Wednesday in August.

Hawkshead Show, Hawkshead – middle Saturday in August

Cartmel Races, Cartmel – Late Summer Bank Holiday weekend.

Kendal Sheepdogs Trials, County Showground, Kendal – end of August.

Kendal Folk Festival, Kendal – a week at the end of August

Cartmel Priory Open Day, Cartmel – one Saturday in August every two years (even numbers).

SEPTEMBER

Westmorland County Show, County Showground, Kendal – 2nd Thursday in September.

Kendal Gathering Kendal – 17 days in late August/early September.

Charter Festival Celebrations, Ulverston – 2 weeks around the 11th of September.

Hot Air Balloon Rally, Holker Hall – a middle Saturday in September.

OCTOBER

Kendal Jazz Festival, Kendal – 2 weeks in October or November

NOVEMBER

Michaelmus Funfair, The Gill, Ulverston – Thursday after the 12th November.

Tourist Information Centres

Kendal
Town Hall, Highgate, Kendal, Cumbria, LA9 4DL.
Tel. (0539) 725758. Open all year.

Grange-over-Sands
Victoria Hall, Main Street, Grange-over-Sands, Cumbria, LA11 6DP.
Tel. (05395) 34026. Open April to October.

Ulverston
Coronation Hall, County Square, Ulverston, Cumbria, LA12 7LZ.
Tel. (0299) 57120. Open all year.

Coniston
16 Yewdale Road, Coniston, Cumbria, LA21 8DU.
Tel. (05394) 41533. Open April to November.

Hawkshead
Main Car Park, Hawkshead, Cumbria, LA22 0NT.
Tel. (05394) 36525. Open April to November.

Bowness-on-Windermere
Glebe Road, Bowness-on-Windermere, Cumbria, LA23 3HJ.
Tel. (05394) 42895. Open April to December.